Six Centuries of
FRENCH MASTER DRAWINGS
in America

Six Centuries of
FRENCH MASTER DRAWINGS
in America

REGINA SHOOLMAN AND CHARLES E. SLATKIN

New York

OXFORD UNIVERSITY PRESS

1950

31721

To FANNY HANNA MOORE *in appreciation and homage*

Preface

It is pleasant to acknowledge once again the friendly assistance of many directors and curators of the museums represented in the following pages, who have invariably been generous of time and patient in supplying documentation. It is hoped that the new information added will be a measure of return for their kindness. Renewed thanks are also due certain scholars and amateurs with whom individual drawings and portions of the text were discussed at length, though responsibility for the final selections and the text rests with the authors. For their early encouragement and later suggestions the authors desire to thank Professor Paul J. Sachs and Miss Agnes Mongan of the Fogg Museum of Art; Mr. Philip Hofer of the Harvard College Library; Professor Frank J. Mather, Jr., of the Princeton University Museum of Historic Art. For advice and helpful suggestions thanks are equally due Mr. Charles Sterling of the Louvre; Miss Elizabeth Mongan of the National Gallery of Art; Miss Louise Burroughs of the Metropolitan Museum; Dr. Walter Friedlander; Drs. E. Tietze-Conrat and Hans Tietze; Dr. Léo Bronstein; Mr. H. P. Rossiter of the Boston Museum; Messrs.

Germain Seligman, Georges de Batz, and Maurice Sloog; and the Duveen and Wildenstein Galleries. To the French Cultural Services, which enabled the authors to study some of the drawing collections in France, thanks are warmly extended. To the owners of private collections whose drawings might ultimately come into museum ownership, acknowledgment of assistance and gracious hospitality is here expressed. For their many courtesies, the authors wish to thank the staff of the Library and the Print Room of the Metropolitan Museum of Art, the Frick Art Reference Library, the Art and Print Room of the New York Public Library and the Pierpont Morgan Library.

Without the unfailing kindness and encouragement of Mrs. Herbert N. Strauss, Mrs. I. C. Stralem, Mrs. Paul Moore, Mrs. Irwin Laughlin, and Miss Belle da Costa Greene, this work could hardly have been completed. More particular thanks are also due the Lucius N. Littauer Foundation for a grant-in-aid, which enabled the authors to carry on their preliminary researches.

REGINA SHOOLMAN
CHARLES E. SLATKIN

Contents

Foreword

'I sit anxiously before the sheet of white paper on which one might say everything, and on which I shall never say more than *some one thing!*'—ANDRÉ GIDE, *Journal*

A SHEET of white paper, indifferent as the void itself—smooth or pebbly, ivory or chalk-white—so long as it remains virgin its texture has no substance. Yet there is nothing richer in latent plenitude than this emptiness, which may be suddenly peopled by all the forms of our imagination. Now the artist lets fall his hand; his pen or his fine brush touches the paper: out of this contact is born a dot, a fragment of a line, a tiny spot. What a metamorphosis! These marks, set down upon the serene amorphous expanse, at once transform it utterly. The sheet now has a center or an axis to which our eye gravitates; and our imagination, alert and expectant, hurries toward that promise of materializing forms. Let the dots be multiplied, let the lines be extended and the little spots made larger: at once the paper acquires a mysterious organization. It will be impossible henceforth to think of it as indifferent; it has left the void, it has been summoned to life, it has a determined existence. For mind and spirit have taken possession of the material object that now becomes the base of a drawn form, its prolongation, its

background. Man has vanquished the vast chaos of endless possibilities—those of his imagination and those of unfathomable matter itself.

Here is perhaps the essential secret of the fascination that drawings exert. Even when they are meticulously finished by a master— that is to say, when it seems to us that no part of them could be altered without injury to the whole—we feel in these complete and seemingly eternal images the very principle of creation: that marvelous and unique *decision* that man, confronted with a universe of forms, has taken—to draw from that universe one form only. And when the drawings are no more than masterly indications, when the dots introduce a rhythm that turns emptiness into measurable space, when the spots radiate aureoles that ripple into the deep shadows like water in a pool, when the lines flow into the premonition of shapes that our eyes continue —then our minds and almost our fingers share in the very mechanism of plastic creation. We are looking on, with inexpressible delight, at the labor and the magic of art. The basic elements of the artist's vision are stripped bare before us, and we can assimilate them much more easily than in painting, where the complex resources of paint, brushwork, and color all unite to conceal the actual inception of the work. If the painter is a colorist or luminist, his drawing will be all a-shimmer with contrasting splashes, with pliant shaded lines; this play of diverse values will reveal an eye sensitive to the intensity of tones according to color and light. If, on the contrary, what the artist sees first is not the union of the form with its setting, but the independent entity of the body itself—in other words, if his vision is that of a sculptor—then his drawing will evoke primarily the relief, the bulk of forms. It may even happen that the artist will betray in his drawings the inner impulses which, for one reason or another, he suppresses in his painting—like Poussin, who in his broad washes pursues a baroque contrast with a vehemence that is never suspected in his paintings of the same period; or like David, whose sketches for the *Tennis-Court Oath*, one of his most rigorous and static compositions, insist upon movement and the mobile play of light—thus bearing witness to an irresistible fondness for a vibrant breathing nature, a fondness that, as a painter, he reveals in his portraits alone.

This facility for the immediate analysis of a painter's way of seeing, which is offered us by the study of drawings, is obviously a sure means to understanding of a whole school of painting. A book on the most beautiful French drawings to be found in public and private collections in the United States—a country where there is so much enthusiasm for French pictures, and where they are collected with such admirable perspicacity—offers

every American an invaluable aid to such understanding, an aid of which there has long been a need. The beautiful plates that fill the following pages are the most acute and subtle guide to the penetration of the French plastic genius.

First of all they enable us to understand what is constant in and peculiar to the French vision. But is there such a thing as an artistic vision determined by a national civilization? It does indeed seem that beyond the personality of every great artist a certain deep-rooted attitude toward man and nature makes itself felt: an attitude toward the resources of imagination and of reality, a way of feeling and seeing that each one of them acquires in the ambiance of a national culture, in contact with the environment in which he lives. There is here some mysterious chemistry of the mind and spirit; it does not depend wholly upon the amount of time the artist spends on his native, or on some foreign, soil, but its result is sufficiently obvious to become an artistic and historic actuality; the deciding factor is the intensity with which the artist's spirit is impregnated by the culture for which he has an affinity. Thus for Poussin and Claude Lorrain, who lived all their mature lives in Italy, the brief years of youth in France were enough to make them paint differently from their Italian contemporaries. Their artistic affiliations are in France, with a David, a Corot; and they did not exercise any important influence in Italy because they did not express the tastes and aspirations of that country. And let us look at two men who came to France from Holland: in the sixteenth century, Corneille of the Hague, called Corneille de Lyon; in the nineteenth century, Van Gogh.

The first drew away from the contemporary Flemish painters of his youth—a Scorel, a Joos van Cleve—and became a typical French portraitist, whose spirited stroke and discreet lyricism make us think of the small portraits Renoir did in his earliest manner. Van Gogh, on the contrary, in spite of all the influence the Impressionists had upon him, in spite of his long stay in France, remained faithful to the Dutch spirit, and his vehement expressionism seems to us a transposition into modern idiom of the heart-rending confessions of Rembrandt.

How can we try to define, simply and in few words, that French *manner of seeing*, which imposed itself upon Corneille and stayed by Poussin and Claude all their lives? When we compare the drawings of French artists to those of painters of other nations, we have the impression that they are rarely so stylized as Italian or German work. 'I like what is called style, but I do not like mannerism; the man who is mannered will not be able to see clearly when he is in front of the model,' David used to say to his pupils. 'Be true first, and noble afterward.' David was a great stylist according to the French conception of that word. On the other hand, it appears that the French do not transcribe nature so faithfully as certain Flemings, certain Dutchmen, or certain Germans. The French draughtsman, in other words, does not wish to turn aside from nature; but neither does he follow it to the letter, to give himself up to it without imposing any corrections of his own. In the words of the painters themselves, in France, and in the writings of critics, two expressions appear and reappear in the consideration of drawings, and usually the two are coupled:

'The difficulty is to make one's work *beautiful* and *natural* in following the model,' repeats David. And Baudelaire, greatest of French art critics, has clearly defined, in his *Curiosités Esthétiques*, that attitude which may seem complex but which is in reality instinctive with the French artist, since it corresponds to the profound aspiration of French civilization, in literature, in costume, in the way of life, toward what is at the same time natural and perfect in form. Baudelaire scorns the drawing that seeks after literal veracity; he calls it silly; he respects the classic drawing (that of Poussin, David, Ingres), in which the artist follows nature but corrects it in order that it may be idealized; he admires the drawing that is freely creative, the work of the imagination that to his eyes is the privilege of genius, but there, too, he cannot do without reference to nature. 'The great quality of the drawing of the supreme artists is the *truth* of motion,' he writes, 'and Delacroix never violates this *natural* law.' Thus even for Baudelaire, one of the most lyric minds that France ever produced, imagination should not play beyond bounds or exercize itself in a vacuum, but must penetrate and exalt nature's truths.

This double concern with truth to nature and with the stylization that embellishes it has been common to all Europe since the theorists of the Renaissance. It often remained merely a theoretic postulate; whereas in France it entered, so to speak, into the artist's blood. It never prevented other schools from going to excess—often itself the mark of genius— in naturalism on the one hand or stylization on the other; whereas in France the artists, in avoiding this excess, only rarely attained the expressive power that is given to those who spontaneously abandon themselves to one of these poles of art. The French have not had such severely constructive stylists of form as Holbein; beside him, Clouet and even Ingres appear to be but gentle modelers of the surface skin. Nor have they had such visionaries of reality as Rembrandt and Goya. Only a few artists, born on the borders of France, breathing an air traversed by Germanic or Italian currents—Callot and Claude, who grew up in Lorraine; Daumier, the Southerner —sometimes made use of powerful contrasts; and they remain exceptional.

The French draughtsman tends, on the whole, toward the union of line with modeling. He tends toward a drawing full of supple pictorial suggestions, one that is not purely linear. As early as the fifteenth century, when the drawing of the Primitives was basically linear, Fouquet was probably the first in Europe to make use of soft chalks of various colors. This technique seems indeed to have been unknown in Italy, insomuch as Leonardo, that mind so avid for novelty, had no knowledge of it and learned about it from a French painter, Jean de Paris. During several centuries it was to contribute to the fame of an uninterrupted line of French *crayonneurs* and pastellists: Clouet, Dumoustier, Vivien, Perronneau, Quentin La Tour, Chardin, Delacroix, Degas, Odilon Redon. In the sixteenth century the Italians brought the technique of supple washes to France, to the school of Fontainebleau; if the French made it their own, and later produced the masterpieces of a Claude, a Fragonard, a Saint-Aubin, it was because, without insisting upon the palpable relief of a figure, it permitted the suggestion

of the living vibration of the modeling, under the caress of light. The limpid and tenuous wash satisfied the essential requirement of French art: not to be obvious. On the other hand, one finds only rarely in France drawings in which the splash of chalk or wash is dominant over the line, in which the line loses its basic function of constructing the form.

Thus the artist seeks a balance of technical means to express his vision, which is concerned at once with mobile life and with a firm and beautiful form. And when this serene equilibrium is handled by masters, when Watteau, Ingres, Degas create with their light sure fingers a body or a face, you would not dream of reproaching them with falling short of the vigor of a Dürer, a Rembrandt, or a Goya. You would not know which to admire more—the warm, familiar life, or the form that satisfies our secret need to see plastic signs arranged in a musical order.

The quest for such a balance, more than the extreme attitudes, needs to take cognizance of itself, to clarify itself little by little, as the hand of the artist is materializing his vision. In such a process, drawing is an irreplaceable aid. It is perhaps for this reason that it played such an important role in French painting. In this school one scarcely knows of any great painter who was not at the same time a great draughtsman: Chardin, and to a lesser degree Courbet, are exceptions to this rule. As for the Spanish school, for instance, it has, with the superb exception of Goya, bequeathed us nothing in drawing that is comparable to the work produced by the brush of Greco, Velasquez, or Zurbaran. On the other hand, it seems that in France, more than in other countries, there were great draughtsmen who were not necessarily great painters. Every century has known them: the Clouets and Dumoustiers in the sixteenth, Callot in the seventeenth, Gabriel de Saint-Aubin in the eighteenth, and finally Guys and even Daumier, whose painting, no matter how beautiful it may be, does not equal his work in drawing. To be sure, Italy had also a Piranesi, Germany a Urs Graf, England a Blake; but they remain more or less isolated, on their high level, in their respective schools. When Impressionism introduced the custom of painting directly from nature, without making preparatory studies, it would have seemed that the great tradition of drawing might be threatened. Indeed, Manet, Monet, and Pissarro did draw relatively little, compared to the masters who had preceded them through the centuries. But this was only a temporary eclipse. Renoir, already, was enthusiastic over drawing, and Cézanne attached great importance to it. With Puvis de Chavannes, Toulouse-Lautrec, Seurat, Gauguin, Van Gogh, and the sculptors Rodin and Maillol, the prestige of drawing was established on higher ground than ever before. The Fauves, with their satellites, have added the masterpieces of Matisse, Rouault, Marquet, Dufy, and Dunoyer de Segonzac. And if the Ecole de Paris, which was made up of painters from all over the world, produced admirable draughtsmen in Picasso, Modigliani, Pascin, and Chagall, it was largely because the tradition of drawing was still deeply rooted in France.

So drawing, in France, seems inseparable from painting. It often, indeed, throws light upon aspects of historic evolution which the study of painting alone does not enable us to perceive or does not openly make manifest. There are certain provincial currents that are made plain only in the work of draughtsmen, but which have an essential part in the development of some great painters. Such, for example, is the case of Watteau, to whom the heritage of Callot's brilliant mannerism had been transmitted by Sébastien Leclerc and Claude Gillot, through their lively drawings with their inflections at once calligraphic and mordant. Sometimes drawing has played a capital role in the development of a new phase of art: the 'Rubenism' and 'Venetianism' of France in the early eighteenth century sprang not only from the contemplation of paintings by Rubens and the Venetian masters but also from the study of the prodigious collections of enthusiastic lovers of drawings who gathered them together by the thousands. It was in copying the drawings of Titian and Veronese in the home of Crozat that Watteau's vision matured; it was then that he grasped the very essence of the picturesque richness of the Venetian draughtsmanship.

For all these reasons, such a book as this one now presented by Regina Shoolman and Charles Slatkin cannot but abound in artistic and historic suggestiveness. The authors supply us with much precise information on the most beautiful French drawings now in America, adding interesting personal comments for the non-specialist. They do not list all of them, because they are too numerous to be brought together in one handy volume, and too unequal in importance to be of general value to the great public that is interested in art. What we have here is a choice. There are still gaps, in American collections, in the earlier periods—that is, in the fifteenth, sixteenth, and seventeenth centuries. But from the time of Watteau on, these collections are so rich that a selection of capital pieces is not an easy task. It is always possible to dispute a choice, just as one may find an author's aesthetic comment too individual; but is thought, especially when applied to art, not always arbitrary? As the value of a work of art rests solely on the choice of one line among a thousand lines, of one spot among all the possible spots that nature offers; as a collection of works of art receives its accent, its forceful significance, only by virtue of the individual taste that has directed the selection of each piece; so a book on art finds its worth only in the decisiveness of the thought which, sometimes in agreement with our ideas and sometimes in opposition to them, unfailingly stimulates our own reflections. In the old days, in France, a drawing was called *une pensée,* 'a thought'—that is to say, an imaginary, ideal concept of a form or a composition. Brought together in such a book as this, these 'thoughts' of the French painters, gathered from five or six centuries, do not only delight our eyes: they become our own thoughts, our own mind's children.

CHARLES STERLING
Conservateur des Peintures, Musée du Louvre.
Foreign Adviser, The Metropolitan
Museum of Art, New York

*(Translated from the French by
Katherine Woods)*

Introduction

DRAWING has traditionally played a useful but auxiliary role in the craft of the painter, at best that of a handmaiden to the more spectacular arts of painting and sculpture, and quite overshadowed by them. It was only in France, as Meder said, that drawing early attained a 'graphic sufficiency . . . lacking in all other nations.'* While medieval French manuscript illustration depended for its full effect upon the lavish use of color, as well as on the linear design that formed its basic structure, the outstanding work of the School of Paris surviving from the fourteenth century is, significantly, a monochrome drawing on silk—the altar cloth known as the *Parement de Narbonne* (Louvre). This anonymous drawing, with its purity and austerity of forms, is in the so-called international style—a fusion of Italian, Flemish, and French elements; but the sentiment of Siena and the realism of Flanders are quite subdued, while the graphic and decorative elements are clearly stated. The *Parement* may thus fairly be considered the first important achievement in a series that earned for French drawing the

*Meder, J., *Handzeichnungen Französischer Meister des XVI-XVIII Jahrhunderts*, Vienna, 1922, p. 5.

prestige of a separate and independent category of art.

It is in the ability to define by means of line alone not only the form but the concept, not only spatial relation, tone, and texture but mood and meaning as well, that France's particular genius is revealed. The qualities that distinguish her draftsmen appear and reappear with a constancy that establishes them as French traits: the suavity of line that relates the Clouet portrait drawings to those of Ingres and Degas; the intense lyrical feeling for nature in the drawing of Claude and Fragonard, Renoir and Dufy; the wit, now fierce, now scintillating, leaping from the droll marginalia of medieval manuscripts to the satiric pens of Callot, Daumier, and Toulouse-Lautrec; and finally, that talent for decorative harmony that redeems the eclecticism of the Fontainebleau School and becomes the primary motive in Boucher and Fragonard, Puvis de Chavannes, and Matisse.

Though closely connected with and often rising out of its sister arts, engraving and etching, drawing in France gradually achieved its self-sufficient role with only incidental reference to painting. The narrative, all-embracing character of fourteenth-century manuscript illustration (Pl. 1) broke down in the succeeding centuries into six separate categories: portrait, figure, landscape, genre, historical (mythological), and architectural drawing. The graphic arts, rather than painting, often determined the predominance of one category over the others: thus, the vogue for medallions and engraved portraits in the sixteenth and seventeenth centuries was paralleled by the development of portrait drawing; while certain reproductive processes —mezzotint, aquatint, et cetera—popularized the use of bistre and sepia, gouache, and wash drawings—excellent media for the free rendering of landscape, which thus gained ascendancy. Callot's etchings, the engravings of Nanteuil and Mellan, the 'chalk-manner' prints after Boucher, and the lithographs of Delacroix and Daumier called for the production of a great number of sketches by these artists. Whether drawn in preparation for a later work or done for its own sake—a graphic notation pointing up the fleeting expression in a face, the contour of a woman's body, the interlacing foliage of trees, the structure of a noble ruin—French drawing inevitably reflects the national predilection for elegance, refinement, lucidity, and logic.

Although the extant drawings of the Fontainebleau School are rare documents of a group of works now almost wholly destroyed or disfigured beyond significance, their æsthetic value is limited. However, the crayon portraiture of the sixteenth century, distinct from the oil studies of the period, presents a solid achievement in the exploitation of a single medium—colored chalk. The artists of the seventeenth century broadened the scope of

drawing until it embraced virtually every medium known to graphic expression. Callot employed pen, pencil, or fine crayon for the swift notation of his thoughts (Pls. 18, 19); Claude relied almost entirely on wash for the luminous effects he attained in rendering the poetry of landscape (Pl. 17); Poussin, interested in both linear composition and chiaroscuro modeling, combined pen and brush drawing with rare skill, evoking the subtlest nuances of tone by his use of bistre (Pls. 14, 15). The portraitist Mellan, intent upon exploring the character of his sitters, depended upon the lucid, incisive stroke of pen or pencil to seize the fugitive expression (Pl. 21). As the *grand style* of Louis XIV crystallized, however, the draftsman combined his media in order to build up an elaborate synthesis. It was not unusual for a drawing to include pencil, ink, charcoal, pastel, and Chinese white—an impressive ensemble, designed to overwhelm the spectator (Pl. 24). Here the draftsman has on his own terms virtually set himself up in competition with the painter.

The Regency saw the creation of the rococo style, which flourished uninterruptedly through the reign of Louis XV. In the production of the new motifs that came into vogue —the arabesques, *chinoiseries*, and *rocailles*, mingling in an efflorescence of ornamental design—drawing, with its particular capacity for fluid grace and delicacy, gained prominence. Gilles-Marie Oppenordt's genius for architectural inventiveness and the rich visual imagination of Claude Gillot and his student, Antoine Watteau, explored and elaborated the possibilities of the new rococo style, adding to its pictorial repertoire figures drawn from every walk of life. The financiers and speculators who had profited from the protracted wars of Louis XIV were keen in their appreciation of this unconventional, highly individual art that, with gay insouciance, turned its back on the grand manner. In thousands of drawings, the principles and archetypes of rococo were illustrated, transforming architecture, mural decoration, furniture, tapestry, and all other objects of eighteenth-century décor. The sketch of the *maître-ornemaniste* became the pattern for the new era.

More than any other artist of his day, Watteau embodied the varied and lively spirit, the youthfulness and *espièglerie* of rococo art. Whatever the medium he chose, he made of drawing an eloquent language, subtle, delicate, yet precise. Having developed a highly original pictorial formula (so useful to his followers, Lancret and Pater), he composed his paintings by combining on-the-spot sketches which, taken from life, lent verisimilitude to the dream world of his painted fancies. But his drawings were never merely reportorial; his virtuosity with colored chalks enabled him to disclose the man behind the actor's face, to expose the quality of a mind in the gesture of a hand (Pl. 25), until for him drawing became a terse and epigrammatic synthesis of the individual and the epoch.

The great decorators Boucher and Fragonard drew incessantly; the fugitive sketch, the preliminary study, or the highly finished drawing that became in their hands an independent art form was executed in a variety of media—red or black chalk, pencil, pen, or wash. Boucher, whose mastery in depicting the nude feminine form was unsurpassed in his

day, often drew from life, although he boasted that the experience gained in his early student days had made it easy enough for him to dispense with models. His life studies—done in red or black chalk, often heightened with white, or in pencil—are far more sincere in their striving for mastery of form than the glib and facile *académies de femme* that his studio produced in enormous quantities to satisfy the ever-growing demand of the new *amateur* class. Fragonard, highly gifted and imaginative in his figure studies and landscapes, knew how to vary the effects obtained from each medium, developing a graphic range that is astonishing. In his wash drawings he approaches the virtuosity of Claude and Tiepolo; his pen and red-chalk studies are intimate, direct, and brilliant observations. 'Chaleur et originalité, c'est ce qui le caractérise,' was David's tribute to him, though the moralists deplored his *sujets galants*, those frankly licentious 'cartoons' that, transcribed by the engraver's tools, became the *estampes galantes* of the day.

Aside from prints, piquant and *grivois*, which titillated the aristocracy and the *bourgeoisie*, the richest source of income for the French draftsman during the eighteenth century was that of book illustration. Fine editions of the works of Molière (1734), Boccaccio's *Decameron* (1757), the *Fables* of La Fontaine (1762), and the *Metamorphoses* of Ovid (1767) were illustrated by the foremost artists. Boucher's drawings for the works of Molière, done with the freshness and verve of a youthful talent, became collectors' items. Eisen, Cochin, and Gravelot produced some of their most spirited and agreeable compositions for publications such as those mentioned, while the drawings that Fragonard and Hubert Robert made as illustrations for the Abbé de Saint-Non's *Voyage pittoresque en Italie* were the most spectacular feature of that ruinously ambitious venture.

The luxurious life at court and the desperately gay aristocracy at play—the concerts, fêtes, theatrical performances, soirées, and extravagant outdoor entertainments—inspired the imagination of the Saint-Aubin brothers, Augustin and Gabriel. Pre-revolutionary Paris rises magically from the pages of their sketch books, its every aspect caught and recorded in graceful, sharply defined vignettes, which strike an uncannily modern note (Pls. 41, 55).

Moreau le Jeune's account of contemporary manners is less impressionistic and more fully documented, belonging actually in the category of genre. One of the most prolific draftsmen in an age that considered drawing an elegant accomplishment, he earned official recognition for the graphic artists of his day by his appointment as *Dessinateur des Menus-Plaisirs du Roi* to Louis XVI. His finest work is the series of plates designed for the *Monument du Costume* (Pl. 56), drawings that retained their full charm and linear suavity in the engraved versions. In the second half of the eighteenth century these plates far outweighed in importance the text accompanying the *suites d'estampes*, which served merely to point up some choice aspect of the engraving.

While Chardin and Greuze extolled the virtues of family life, the former in his infrequent, carefully composed studies, the latter in sketches of enormous vitality and freedom, some of their contemporaries—Baudouin, Lavreince, Debucourt—almost as gifted but catering to an age of *libertins*, drew for the

market of the *estampes galantes*. Accomplished masters of calligraphic form and movement, they combined with sly ambiguity genre scenes of playful innocence and suggestive innuendo.

For Ingres drawing was a means of arriving at truth through form restored to classic dignity. Hundreds of sketches for important compositions such as the *Martyrdom of St. Symphorien* (Pl. 65) attest to his ceaseless struggle to master in line the complex rhythms and relations of diverse elements, rendered with a classic harmony that was for him the highest form of artistic expression.

It was on the strength of David's early drawings that Boucher recommended a painter's career for the future dictator of the arts. Drawings are often the first sign of revolt, the preliminary experiments toward a new style and point of view. David, along with most of the eighteenth-century graphic artists, espoused the cause of the Revolution, sensing the social decay beneath the court life they portrayed. To the men of his generation the rococo style symbolized the *ancien régime,* and with them the playful vagaries of rococo draftsmanship were transformed into disciplined, classic design. Nicolas Poussin became the revered ancestor, emulated by David in his many studies inspired by the antique. As in Poussin's, there is an emotional quality in David's drawings that becomes firmly controlled and rationalized in his paintings.

Modern artists often paint as members of a school or movement, but they draw as solitaries. That the painters of the Romantic movement should reveal themselves most fully and intimately in their drawings was, of course, inevitable. These personal, immediate expressions, not intended to demonstrate a particular doctrine, as did their paintings, were the artists' unguarded thoughts. The strong influence of Spain in the work of Courbet and Manet is hardly to be found in their drawings. Men as similar in their paintings as Monet, Pissarro, Bonnard, and Segonzac are essentially dissimilar in their drawings. Pissarro in his paintings is allied to the Impressionists; in his themes he follows Millet; but his method of drawing is largely his own. Corot's paintings have much in common with those of Courbet, but the drawings of both artists are wholly unlike. The expressionism of Van Gogh and Gauguin is tempered in their drawings. Hence the great diversity that is found in nineteenth- and twentieth-century French painting becomes further individualized in the drawings of that period.

There was a common tendency toward polarity and antithesis, an insistence on arriving at corresponding ends by opposite means. The romantic intransigeance of Delacroix and Géricault had its counterpart in the sedate traditionalism of Millet. Ingres's linear purity, brilliantly apt for achieving a poised and pulsating immobility, was adapted by Degas to seize casual movement; and then the immobility was restored, but without Ingres's supple resilience of contour, in the mysterious calm and hieratic elegance of Seurat's world. Millet's rugged peasants are to be found trapped and brutalized in the city, where Daumier pried at their sores and frailties. The static figures of Millet's eclogues gave way to animated realism in Daumier's scenes, the imposing masses of the former attenuated into slashing lines of satire in the latter. In other sketches a rich vitality was achieved by the very accident of Daumier's

crumbling crayon, which, as it gave way under the driving pressure of his fingers, was twisted to the sharp edge as the line needed refining, or was broadened to a stub that was quickly pressed into service for tell-tale nuances of shading, swirls of movement that failed of neat precision but arrived instead at a greater suggestibility. Intent on a similar realism, Corot, cautious, painfully slow and deliberate, worked with steel-like pencil point, seeking out the precise lines that are not in nature but in man's image of her. These literal transcriptions of Corot, who wished to leave nothing to chance or memory, contrast with the 'divine memory' of Daumier and his rapid sketches, and with the middle approach of Degas, who felt that the best method was to 'fill your eye' with the model and then dash up to the attic to do the sketch, unhampered by the original.

This truth to substance was in turn countered by other artists in their insistence on the truth to transitory surface appearances, since the very nature of objects, suffused in ever-changing light and shade, is altered by the fleeting glimmer and sparkle of glancing lights. Monet, Renoir, and Seurat sought to render these effects in black and white as well as in color. For these men the ultimate source of reality lay in the scientific laws of optics. Then the flux and movement in the momentary images of Monet or Pissarro were stilled and held fast by Signac and Seurat at a time when the entire Impressionist thesis was being opposed by yet another approach. Renoir's later search for soft textures and glimmering contours was followed by Cézanne's probing for the hidden essences below the surface, the cubic density beyond the surface appearance;

while elsewhere Gauguin and Van Gogh were collapsing perspective into flat surface patterns and masses of black-and-white harmonies in the manner of Oriental design.

It was a period of diversity, of ambivalence, and of paradox. If the heyday of the French Revolution nurtured classicism, in its failing days it gave new life to romanticism, whose spirit of revolt was dramatized in themes of brutality and horror taken from everyday life. Naturalism in Corot and Millet was born of an impulse toward mysticism, while realism itself, in Degas and Toulouse-Lautrec, took to the most romantic retreats. The romantic exoticism of the Near East was abandoned for the greater truth of the Far East, borrowing method rather than subject matter. Except for the persistent influence of the classic tradition and Ingres, no overwhelming authority manifested itself beyond the scientific preoccupations and the impulse toward every facet of realism. Japanese influence, which was strong in the late nineteenth century, spread in the twentieth into a dispersal of sources of inspiration that was almost universal in time and space: modern Africa and ancient Greece in the work of the Spaniard Picasso, the medieval in Rouault, the Italian primitives in Modigliani, the Near East in Matisse. The greatest talent was that of Degas, the greatest heart that of Daumier, the most disciplined intellect that of Seurat, the profoundest spirit, Rouault's, while the most representative modern figure, embracing the multiplicity of interests and the newer science and psychology, was that of the expatriate Picasso. Special interests ranged from the Biblical dramas of Millet to the exoticism of Gauguin, from the irony of Forain to the sardonic realism of Toulouse-

Lautrec or the surrealism of Redon; and techniques, from the structural masses of Guys to the frail sinuousness of Dufy.

Matisse has said that a drawing consists not only of what is set down but also of what is not; the pen moves and the artist is forever committed as surely as the speaker or writer. Often he will draw out of sheer physical need to empty himself of certain moods or responses, out of a condition of restless discomfort that impedes his progress in oil. So the artist may compulsively return again and again to certain lines and configurations until he reaches a point of satiety. He can then proceed with equilibrium. Millet, like Matisse, found so much that needed recording as mood or inventive thought that only by using pencil or charcoal could he find enough time to satisfy his need. Often the artist turns to the pencil to check the data that his senses provide or to train his hand to obey his eyes and at the same time to instruct his eyes in what the automatic muscular response to the scene or image produces. Thus the artist himself often comes to gaze at his handiwork in astonished delight and admiration.

The rapidly increasing number of publications devoted to drawings, which have recently appeared on this side of the ocean—those of Ingres, Seurat, Renoir, Géricault, Robinson, Grosz, and so on—suggests a concern for the thought processes and techniques of the artist beyond a formal interest in his paintings. Of this interest there is further evidence in the record of exhibitions and bibliography in the catalogue notes that follow.

Of master drawings in American collections there are perhaps more of the French school than of all others combined. To select the best of this rich variety and at the same time to illustrate the full development of the school through six centuries, to suggest the range of the major artists' work as well as the scope of the various collections in just proportion, must inevitably involve many compromises. Certain often reproduced masterpieces could not well be omitted, yet fresh and little known works were happily to be found in abundance. Most gratifying is the opportunity to tie in with the best drawings from the major centers examples scattered in collections too limited in size to warrant separate publication. Thus where only two or three museums have had occasion to study and publish a catalogue of their drawings, the present survey brings together from over two score different sources some of the outstanding examples, here assembled in interrelated and orderly progression, so that isolated masterpieces in remote cities may be readily examined within a chronological setting. Because of limited space, certain magnificent drawings by the great masters had to give way to fine works by lesser artists, and the work of several significant artists had to be foregone altogether. A well-known author has said that he judges the quality of his work by the excellence of the material that he finally deletes. This book might fairly be judged by that dictum, for the omissions themselves could only have added confirmation to what is here amply demonstrated: the extraordinary fertility of France's graphic genius, her unflagging energy in creating new forms and ever-fresh linear definitions of exquisite grace and refinement, which have perhaps been excelled only by the early Florentines. It is a matter of

regret that the fragile nature of drawings is such that only occasional exhibitions can be shown and rarer loans made by museums and galleries; but they are available for study by the individual, and such publications as this may serve to stimulate their study. It was the authors' privilege to examine almost all of these collections, though in certain instances drawings were framed and their removal to examine signatures and inscriptions was not permitted.

That so choice and extensive a gathering of master drawings should now be housed and cared for in our scattered neighborhoods is largely owing to the talents and tastes of a limited number of individuals. The painter Smibert is said to have brought certain drawings with him from Italy in the early eighteenth century; and the Honorable James Bowdoin in 1813 bequeathed to Bowdoin College an interesting group of drawings he had purchased in France. At about the same time, J. G. Cogswell gathered in Europe a number of drawings that later formed part of Mortimer Schiff's fine collection. The artist William Morris Hunt bought a number of fine Barbizon School drawings and stressed their value in his art classes; his friend Quincy Adams Shaw built up a major collection of Millets, now in the Boston Museum. In recent times Cornelius Vanderbilt and Cephas G. Thompson acquired superb collections of drawings that are now in our museums. One of the most extensive single purchases was that of the C. Fairfax Murray collection bought by J. Pierpont Morgan and now in the library that bears his name; a number of excellent additions have since been made by the present administration of the library. The largest collection of drawings, some thirty thousand papers, primarily architectural and decorative-arts sketches, including the famous Decloux collection of Paris, is now at the Cooper Union Museum. Of French drawings, one of the richest groups was acquired by H. O. Havemeyer, most of these having since gone to the Metropolitan Museum. A choice collection of modern French drawings is at the Museum of Modern Art, a good number through the bequest of Lillie P. Bliss. The dispersal of the great collections of the Marquis de Biron, J. P. Heseltine, Marius Paulme, David-Weill, Louis Roederer, and Henry Oppenheimer resulted in the acquisition by American collectors and museums of some of the outstanding drawings.

A number of serious students and amateurs, men of means and taste, of sensibility and discernment, have more recently enriched our collections; among them are Grenville Winthrop, Paul J. Sachs, and Charles Loeser, whose superb collections have gone to the Fogg Museum; Professor F. J. Mather, Jr. and Dan Fellows Platt of Princeton University; Mrs. Gustave Radeke and Mrs. Murray S. Danforth of Providence, Rhode Island; Lessing Rosenwald of Jenkintown, Pennsylvania; Mrs. Lenora Hall Gurley and Mr. and Mrs. Charles Worcester of Chicago. The stimulation of interest in drawing has stemmed largely from the Fogg Museum of Art, whose students, under the guidance of Professors Paul J. Sachs and Jakob Rosenberg, have in scattered communities undertaken to fire enthusiasm and encourage amateurs and collectors, so that often the most unexpected communities in out-of-the-way regions are possessors of important or rare master drawings, which are being enjoyed by ever-increasing numbers.

Many of the drawings discussed in the following pages have no bibliography or have previously been simply reproduced but not studied. A considerable task of research remains to be done on innumerable drawings, acquired sometimes in lots, and now stored in museums whose staffs are too limited, or preoccupied with administrative duties, or remote from the necessary library and other research facilities to undertake the necessary study and to separate the valuable works. To this problem of identification and attribution the present study is in part intended as an aid.

Six Centuries of
FRENCH MASTER DRAWINGS
in America

ABBREVIATIONS

Royal Academy, *Catalogue, French Art*   *Commemorative Catalogue, Exhibition of French Art*, 1200-1900, Royal Academy of Arts, London, 1932.

C. Fairfax Murray   Murray, C. Fairfax, *Drawings by Old Masters in the Collection of J. Pierpont Morgan*, London, 1910-12, 4 vols.

Mongan and Sachs   Mongan, A. and Sachs, P. J., *Drawings in the Fogg Museum of Art*, Cambridge, 1940, 3 vols.

Lavallée   Lavallée, P., *Le Dessin français du XIIIe au XVIe siècle*, Paris, 1931.

Heseltine   Heseltine, J. P., *Dessins de l'école française du dix-huitième siècle*, Paris, 1913.

David-Weill   Henriot, G., *Collection David-Weill*, Paris, 1928, 3 vols.

Pl. 1

FRENCH SCHOOL
Early Fifteenth Century

Grandes Chroniques de France

Pen and ink on vellum; 14½ x 11 in. (367 x 279 mm.) *Date:* 1400-1410.

WALTERS ART GALLERY, Baltimore, Md.

Collections: Lemaire de Flicourt; Duc de la Rochefoucauld.

Bibliography: Ricci, S. de, and Wilson, W. J., *Census of Medieval and Renaissance Manuscripts in the United States and Canada*, New York, 1935, p. 850, no. 523.

The fifteenth century saw the last flowering of Gothic art in France. Man's keen awareness of and delight in the mundane aspects of life are the theme upon which the artist played his variations. The world of the senses was mirrored in color; but its energy and vitality were expressed in line, which now abandoned its diagrammatic character and became supple, rhythmic, and fluent. The drawing for the *Grandes Chroniques* at the Walters Art Gallery exemplifies only one phase of the rich diversity of styles current in the fifteenth century. The compact design and tightness of line betray the artist's dependence on the ivory-carver's formula, his inability to free himself from an effect of bas-relief surfaces. This drawing, however, is more static, far less tormented in feeling than the carved ivories that dominated French art forms during the preceding century. The narrative style, which the anonymous artist of the Walters Art Gallery *Chronicles* has handled with some timidity, was to find its complete expression in the miniatures of Jean Fouquet.

Pl. 2

JEAN FOUQUET

1420-1480

Portrait of a Papal Legate

Silver point; 7 13/16 x 5¼ in. (199 x 135 mm.) Inscribed, upper right: *Ung Roumain legat de nostre St pere en france.*

METROPOLITAN MUSEUM OF ART, New York, N. Y.

Collections: Prosper Lanckrink; J. P. Heseltine; H. Oppenheimer; Duveen.

Bibliography: Bouchot, H., *Exposition des primitifs français*, Paris, 1904, pl. 38. Lafenestre, G., *Jehan Foucquet*, Paris 1905, p. 71, reproduced p. 27. Friedlaender, M. J., *Prussian Yearbook*, Berlin, 1910, vol. XXXI, pp. 227-30, reproduced. Cox, T., *Jehan Foucquet*, London, 1931, p. 133, reproduced. Lavallée, p. 70, pl. XIX. Royal Academy, *Catalogue, French Art*, no. 541, pl. 626. Perls, K., *Jean Fouquet*, Paris, 1941, p. 22, reproduced p. 252.

Exhibited: Paris, 'Exposition des primitifs français,' 1904. London, Burlington House, 'French Art, 1200-1900,' 1932, no. 541. San Francisco, Golden Gate International Exposition, 'Master Drawings,' 1940.

Emanating from the region midway between Italy and Flanders, the art of France is a logical fusion of the salient qualities that appear in the art of her neighbors. Directly fed by these inspirational sources, the work of Jean Fouquet of Tours combines the monumentality and idealism of the one with the closely observed realism of the other. But beyond these, and more important, Fouquet happily gives distinct and full expression to the elegance and refinement, the lyricism and pictorial wit, which come to be distinguishing and recurrent traits in French art. Certain of these qualities are evidenced in the superb *Portrait of a Papal Legate*: the sturdy visage, the keen, purposeful gaze, and the compressed determination of the lips are those of an imposing man of affairs. Lacking are the homelier qualities, the idiosyncrasies that commonly mark those personalities of the Loire country, which Fouquet caught with such immediacy of effect. The drawing of the costume itself is unexpectedly dull, and on several other counts the authorship of the drawing has been disputed. Yet there is an elegance and fastidiousness that mark it as French, and it is not inconceivable that it should have come from the hand of the greatest master of that day. The subject is believed to be Teodor Lelli, Bishop of Treviso, who, in the capacity of Papal Legate, visited France in 1464.

Pl. 3

SCHOOL OF FONTAINEBLEAU

FRANCESCO PRIMATICCIO

1504-1570

Recto: *The Birth of Adonis;* Verso: *Penelope and Ulysses*

Ink; recto: 14½ x 20 in. (367 x 500 mm.); verso: 5½ x 12 in. (143 x 312 mm.)

MUSEUM OF HISTORIC ART, PRINCETON UNIVERSITY, Princeton, N. J.

Collections: Manteau; Marquis de Chennevières; Seligman.

Having officially launched the Renaissance in France, François I sought to nourish it with the presence and the creative activities of Italy's greatest living masters, whom he invited to decorate his palace at Fontainebleau. In the end he had to content himself with lesser men: Rosso the Florentine, follower of Michelangelo and Pontormo; and Primaticcio, assistant and follower of Raphael's student, Giulio Romano. Eclectic and mannerist in style, subject to varying influences, as artists of lesser talents are, Rosso and Primaticcio soon adapted their work to the French taste for elegance and decorative harmony. Under Henri II and his Italian consort Catherine de Medici, the Fontainebleau School continued after Rosso's death to flourish under the leadership of Primaticcio, who, with the assistance of Niccolo del Abbate, carried out an extensive series of decorations in the Ballroom and in the Ulysses Gallery. A number of Primaticcio's original drawings (Louvre, Chantilly) are the only surviving records of the since vanished frescoes.

The Birth of Adonis and, more especially, the drawing of Penelope and Ulysses on the reverse side were apparently done in preparation for these frescoes, though they may possibly be engraver's copies. The figures of Penelope and Ulysses on the *verso* appear, with some variations, in a painting of the Fontainebleau School now in the Earl of Carlyle Collection (Dimier, L., *Le Primatice*, Paris, 1928, pl. XXXVI) while on the *recto* (in the foreground) the seated nymph playing the flute bears a stylistic resemblance to the figure of Danae at Chantilly (Dimier, pl. IX). The story here told is of the Cyprian princess Myrrha, who, changed into a myrtle tree, gave birth to the infant Adonis, beloved of nymphs and muses who rejoiced over him. In both studies, so different in style and workmanship, the fragile, elongated figures with their expressive hands and feet, the melodious flow of the composition, the refined and gracious conception of the theme may be recognized as distinguishing traits of the Fontainebleau School.

6

Pl. 4

JACQUES ANDROUET DU CERCEAU THE ELDER

c.1510-c.1584

Isometric Perspective Drawing of the Château de Verneuil

Ink and watercolor; 16⅞ x 21½ in. (428 x 546 mm.) *Date:* 1568-1575.

Cooper Union Museum for the Arts of Decoration, New York, N. Y.

Collections: Destailleur; Decloux.

Bibliography: Geymuller, Baron H. de, *Les Du Cerceau*, Paris, 1887, pp. 82-6, fig. 41. *Dessins originaux provenant de la collection de M. H. Destailleur, Paris,* 1896, no. 159.

Exhibited: New York, Architectural League, '27th Annual Exhibition,' 1911; New London, Conn., Lyman Allyn Museum, 'Drawings,' 1936, no. 49.

With Henri II the French Renaissance reached its apogee. The idiom of the Italian Renaissance had been grasped and assimilated by men like Pierre Lescot, Jean Goujon, and Philibert de l'Orme, who proceeded to create such French monuments as the first wing of the Louvre and the Château d'Anet. Outstanding among the architects of this period was Jacques Androuet Du Cerceau the Elder, who combined the skill of the draftsman with that of engraver, devoting his talents, after a sojourn in Italy, to the task of disseminating his knowledge of the Renaissance style. Commissioned by Henri II to make a series of engravings of the most beautiful buildings in France, Du Cerceau produced his two-volume work, *Les Plus Excellents Bâtiments de France* (1576, 1579), a precise record aimed principally at an elucidation of the new style. The view of the Château de Verneuil, formerly at Verneuil-sur-Oise, near Senlis, may have been drawn by Du Cerceau in preparation for the engraved plate that appears with some variations in *Les Plus Excellents Bâtiments de France,* or it may actually be his architectural drawing for a building he is believed to have planned (cf. Geymuller, op. cit. p. 83). The drawing is notable for the precision of its penwork and for a breadth of treatment unhampered by insistence upon minute detail. Other notable examples of Du Cerceau's workmanship may be seen at the Pierpont Morgan Library.

Pl. 5

JEAN DE GOURMONT

1506-*c.*1551

The Flagellation

Pen and bistre, washed; 8⁹⁄₁₆ x 12¹¹⁄₁₆ in. (218 x 322 mm.)

PIERPONT MORGAN LIBRARY, New York, N. Y.

Collections: Robinson; C. Fairfax Murray.

Bibliography: C. Fairfax Murray, vol. III, no. 66. Lavallée, p. 91. Du Colombier, P., *L'Art renaissance en France,* Paris, 1945, fig. 113.

While the artists working under royal command at Fontainebleau were adapting Italian mannerism to French taste, those independent of the court were acquiring their knowledge of Italian art through engravings. It was through the latter that Jean de Gourmont, printer, engraver, painter, and etcher, active in Paris and Lyons, became familiar with the Renaissance masters. His drawings and engravings, rare and little known today, for the most part Biblical scenes set against architectural backgrounds or Roman interiors, show his preoccupation with the problems of perspective. His success with the series of columns and alternating archways in *The Flagellation* is only moderate. The central drama is curiously subordinated to a concern with posed figures, like those in Pollaiuolo's *Fighting Nudes* (Fogg Museum) and related to the archaic studies of Mantegna. The meticulous workmanship and careful modeling, suggestive of the metal-worker's craft, are found also in a related drawing by Gourmont at the Louvre (see Lavallée, op. cit.) and in his engraved version of *The Flagellation* (Robert-Dumesnil, vol. VII, p. 21, no. 4), which differs considerably from the drawing.

Pl. 6

FRANÇOIS CLOUET

*c.*1510-1572

King François II of France as Dauphin

Black and red crayon; 12⅛ x 8⅝ in. (315 x 213 mm.) *Date: c.*1553. Inscribed in sixteenth-century hand: *le roi françois secom.*

(Gift of Mr. and Mrs. Philip Hofer), HARVARD COLLEGE LIBRARY, Cambridge, Mass.

Collections: Hodgkins; Wickert.

Bibliography: Maumené et d'Harcourt, 'Iconographie des rois de France,' *Archives de l'art français,* n.s., xv, 1928, p. 163. Mongan, A., 'New Clouets at Cambridge,' *Art News,* March 1946, p. 70.

As Queen of France, Catherine de Medici was the country's foremost art patron. Although she preferred the work of her own countrymen, she gave employment to scores of talented French artists, commissioning numerous likenesses of her children and courtiers, so that credit for popularizing portrait drawings generally goes to her, although the tradition had been well established in France for half a century. Preserved in albums and often inscribed with the name of the sitter, thousands of these drawings are today scattered throughout European and American collections. Some have been ascribed with certainty to the known masters of the sixteenth century, chief among whom were Jean and François Clouet. The drawing of Catherine's eldest son, François, is one of the subtlest and most distinguished examples of sixteenth-century portraiture. It shows a freer and more expressive handling than the drawing of the same subject in the Bibliothèque Nationale (dated by Dimier *c.*1553, *Le Dessin français du XVIe siècle,* pl. XXVII). It is easy to understand Catherine de Medici's concern for this delicate boy who ruled but one year and died at sixteen, leaving his young widow Mary Stuart to her tragic destiny.

Pl. 7

FRANÇOIS CLOUET

*c.*1510-1572

Elizabeth, Daughter of Henri II

Black and red crayon; 14 x 8⅞ in. (363 x 230 mm.) *Date: c.*1559. Inscribed, lower left: *Margarite* and the number '34' in an old hand. Collector's mark, lower right: Paul I of Russia.

RICHARD C. PAINE, Chestnut Hill, Mass.

Collections: Cobenzl; The Hermitage, Leningrad; Robert Treat Paine II.

Bibliography: Moreau-Nélaton, E., *Crayons français à Chantilly,* Paris, 1910, vol. I, p. 96. *Les Clouets et leurs émules,* Paris, 1924, vol. II, p. 87; vol. III, fig. 37. Dimier, L., *Histoire de la peinture de portrait en France au XVIe siècle,* Paris, 1925, vol. II, p. 118, no. 34. *Catalogue, C. G. Boerner Sale,* Leipzig, April 1931.

Exhibited: Buffalo, N. Y., Albright Art Gallery, 'Master Drawings,' 1935, no. 34.

Among the crayon drawings ascribed to François Clouet, many exist in several versions, and the task of determining which is the original is likely to be a thankless one, since copies were made in the artist's studio, often by the same hand. The serious child, whose portraits at Chantilly, in the Hermitage, and the Paine collections have been variously considered the original Clouet drawing, was a sister of the dauphin François (see pl. 6) and afterwards Queen of Spain. (cf. Moreau-Nélaton, *Crayons Français,* pl. XLI; and Dimier, II, p. 118, no. 35.) Because of its particular fineness, subtlety, and reticence, the Paine drawing is the one given by Dimier to the original hand of the master.

The Toledo Museum of Art owns one of the few generally accepted works by François Clouet, a beautiful portrait of Elizabeth, done at about the same age.

Pl. 8

FRANÇOIS CLOUET

*c.*1510-1572

Portrait of an Unknown Man

Black and red crayon; 12⅝ x 9 1/16 in. (320 x 230 mm.) *Date: c.*1555. *Watermark:* A small crown (not in Briquet) ; W. 70. Inscribed, upper left: '*No. 5*' and *deborie.*

Fogg Museum of Art, Cambridge, Mass.

Collections: Ignatius Hugford; Marquis de Biron; Alphonse Kann; Paul J. Sachs.

Bibliography: Moreau-Nélaton, E., *Les Clouets et leurs émules,* Paris, 1924, vol. II, p. 96, fig. 357; vol. III, p. 147. Mongan and Sachs, vol. I, pp. 300-301; vol. III, fig. 284, reproduced.

Exhibited: Buffalo, N. Y., Albright Art Gallery, 'Master Drawings,' 1935, no. 33. New London, Conn., Lyman Allyn Museum, 'Drawings,' 1936, no. 50.

The royal house of France, with its courtiers, soldiers, high functionaries, and beautiful women, survives in the portrait drawings of the sixteenth century. When not inscribed with the name of the sitter, many of these have been identified through contemporary paintings and medals, but others remain tantalizingly unknown. The *Portrait of an Unknown Man,* ascribed to the court painter François Clouet, bears the enigmatic inscription *deborie.* This has been thought a possible variant spelling of Claude Gouffier de Boisy, an important court official and patron of François Clouet. Comparison with a painting of de Boisy at Versailles (Moreau-Nélaton, E., *Les Clouets* . . . , vol. II. pl. 457) and with another formerly in the Charles Brunner collection (Paris) adds weight to this assumption, for here is the same austere and melancholy face, aged by some ten years. The strong modeling of the face, unusual in Clouet's work, suggests the possibility that this drawing might be by someone in his immediate circle.

deborié

Pl. 9

FRANÇOIS POURBUS THE YOUNGER
1569-1622

Portrait of Marie de Medici

Black and red chalk; 12 x 8 in. (312 x 208 mm.)
Date: c.1609.

(Huntington Memorial Collection)
CALIFORNIA PALACE OF THE LEGION OF HONOR,
San Francisco, Calif.

Exhibited: Oakland, Calif., Mills College Art
Gallery, 'Old Master Drawings,' 1937,
no. 18. San Francisco, Golden Gate
International Exposition, 'Master
Drawings,' 1940, no. 26 (as *Gabrielle
d'Estrées*).

Presumably a portrait of Gabrielle d'Estrées by
Daniel Dumoustier, this drawing bears no resemblance to the charming mistress of Henri IV (*cf.*
Dreux du Rodier, *L'Europe Illustré*, Paris, 1755,
and Pauquet, H., *Bureaux des modes et costumes
historiques*, Paris, n.d. pl. 38, for Thomas de Leu's
engraving after Daniel Dumoustier). There can
be no doubt, however, that the portrait represents
Marie de Medici, wife of Henri IV (*cf.* Rubens'
Head of Marie de Medici, Victoria and Albert Museum, *Old Master Drawings*, vol. XI, June 1936, pl.
18), who came to France at seventeen, and for ten
years fulfilled her role as queen to a monarch whose
amorous adventures had become legend. After the
death of Henri IV she became Regent until Richelieu exiled her. She died in Cologne in 1642. The
sober naturalism of the drawing suggests the hand
of a Flemish portraitist at the French Court, in all
likelihood François Pourbus the Younger. Of Flemish origin, in 1611 he became court painter to Marie
de Medici. His skillful but rather dry talents, adapted to the prevailing French taste for elegance and
courtliness, were shaped by the tradition of French
crayon portraiture, so that his work after 1611 may
be considered a product of that school. The same
qualities of precision that distinguish his full-length
portrait of the queen (Louvre) are here in evidence.

16

Pl. 10

NICOLAS LAGNEAU
Active c.1575-c.1625

Portrait of a Man

Black chalk heightened with colored chalk on
cream paper; 10¾ x 7½ in. (274 x 191 mm.)

WADSWORTH ATHENEUM, Hartford, Conn.

Collections: Rodrigues.

Bibliography: Catalogue, *Dessins anciens . . . avec
. . . de portraits par Lagneau*, F.
Muller, Amsterdam, 1921, no. 224
(as *Portrait d'un Jeune Artiste*).

Exhibited: Paris, Bibliothèque Nationale, 'Exposition de portraits peints et dessinés du
XIIIᵉ au XVIIᵉ siècle,' 1907, no. 495.

In vivid contrast to the polished court portraiture,
in which sixteenth-century France excelled, is a
group of drawings of plebeian character, dating
from the first half of the seventeenth century. Unknown and unchronicled, this collection of portly
burghers, toothless peasants, jovial ostlers, and
country girls has been attributed to Nicolas Lagneau, who is believed to have come from the Low
Countries. The hundreds of drawings thus bracketed
have some general points of resemblance: a frank
realism often exaggerated into caricature; a preference for the lower social strata; a Calvinist
simplicity of dress and sobriety of mien. Despite
these common traits, the drawings should not be
given to a single artist, so different are their technical aspect and psychological characterization (cf.
Guiffrey, J., and Marcel, P., *L'Inventaire général
des dessins du Musée du Louvre et du Musée de
Versailles*, vol. VII, p. 72).

Lacking the linear play so conspicuous in one
group and the grotesqueness of the other, the *Portrait of a Man* stands apart from the drawings of
the period; in its warm characterization of an
energetic personality, and in the plasticity achieved
by strong modeling in black chalk, it is quite
exceptional.

Pl. 11

PIERRE DUMOUSTIER THE ELDER

c.1540-c.1600

Portrait of Henri I d'Orléans, Duc de Longueville

Black and red crayon, touches of watercolor; 15 x 11½ in. (381 x 291 mm.) *Date:* 1586. Inscribed, upper right: *Aetatis suae 18 an.*

THE DUMBARTON OAKS COLLECTION, Washington, D. C.

Collections: Count G. de Monbrison; Eugène Kraemer.

Bibliography: Sales Catalogue, *Collections Eugène Kraemer, 3e vente*, Galerie Georges Petit, Paris, 2-5 June, 1913, p. 121, no. 148, pl. opposite p. 120. Moreau-Nélaton, E., *Les Clouets et leurs émules*, Paris, 1924, vol. III, p. 153, no. 116 (as *inconnu*).

Stemming from Geoffroy, court painter to Henri II, the Dumoustier brothers, Etienne and Pierre, were favored by Catherine de Medici, who sent them on diplomatic missions to foreign courts. Both made a specialty of portraiture, and the composed mien of their sitters often belied the turbulent, madcap careers of these carousing lords and ladies whose scandalous antics are recorded with such hair-raising fidelity in Brantôme's chronicles. An accomplished draftsman, Pierre Dumoustier the Elder is less dry and literal than his brother Etienne, and also interprets the character of his subjects more penetratingly. The shrewd psychological revelation in the *Portrait of Henri I d'Orléans*, the stylistic treatment of hair and the firm modeling clearly mark it as from the hand of Pierre. In 1586 (the inscription date) Henri was about to distinguish himself in the Wars of Religion.

Pl. 12

DANIEL DUMOUSTIER

1574-1646

Portrait of a Man

Black and red chalk, touches of watercolor; 11⅛ x 9⅝ in. (282 x 243 mm.) Collector's mark, lower right: H. Detmold.

MRS. C. I. STRALEM, New York, N. Y.

Collections: Detmold; Lebeuf de Montgermont; Paulme.

Bibliography: Catalogue des dessins anciens . . . Collection Marius Paulme, Paris, 1929, no. 65, pl. 45.

Despite the countless crayon portraits here and abroad that bear the Dumoustier label, the number of definitely authenticated works by the various members of the Dumoustier family is quite small. Yet the individual method and approach of these few are so strikingly different as to permit by inference and stylistic analysis the classification of many others hitherto loosely grouped under the generic 'Dumoustier Family.'

The portrait of this soldier and dandy, wearing a silk scarf over his armor, a high lace ruff and gold earring, is believed to be by Daniel Dumoustier, who with his cousin, Pierre the Younger, represents the third generation of this family of painters. Rooted in the Clouet tradition, the work of Daniel Dumoustier is wholly confined to portraiture; his sitters included not only the Valois kings, their families and mistresses, but many members of the well-to-do bourgeoisie. It can well be said of Daniel Dumoustier, as it was of Ingres three centuries later, that 'no portraitist was ever franker than he in his characterization; and yet none succeeded so well in gracing his sitters, simply by the brilliance of his method, with a certain elegance.'

Pl. 13

FRANÇOIS QUESNEL
1544-1619

L'Abbé d'Etremont

Black and red chalk; 13⅜ x 9 1/16 in. (340 x 230 mm.) *Date: c.*1587.
Inscribed on back in old hand: *M l'abbé d'Etremont.*

Mrs. Herbert N. Straus, New York, N. Y.

Collections: Févret de Fontette; Sir Francis Douse; Germain Seligman.

Bibliography: Dimier, L., *Douze Crayons de François Quesnel provenant des Collections Fontette, Supplément à l'Histoire de la peinture de portrait en France au XVIe siècle,* Paris, 1927, no. 5, pl. 2. Gerles, G. de, 'Les Crayons français du XVIe siècle du Cabinet Fontette,' *Gazette des Beaux-Arts,* May 1927, pp. 311-16, reproduced facing p. 315.

Exhibited: Buffalo, N. Y., Albright Art Gallery, 'Master Drawings,' 1935, no. 35.

Halfway between the refined psychological portraiture of the Clouets and the robust realism of the Dumoustiers stands the work of François Quesnel. Like his younger brother Nicolas, he inherited his talent from his father, Pierre Quesnel, who had come to Scotland in the retinue of Mary of Guise, wife of James V and mother of Mary Stuart. On their return to France, the Quesnel family secured the patronage of the royal House, François becoming the favorite painter of Henri III. The short and fantastic reign of this dissolute son of Catherine de Medici was marked by a refinement of taste and affectation of manner beneath which ran a current of immorality and sinister fanaticism often ill-concealed in the portraits of the day. François Quesnel hints at the paradoxical nature of this society; his elegent noblemen are reticently drawn, yet one detects their arrogance and venery. The Abbé d'Etremont is clearly a man not wholly devoted to clerical pursuits alone; the sensual mouth and appraising eyes, the cynical lift of the brow are defined by the artist in bold lines that contradict those of the austerely simple costume, while a note of melancholy pervades the study as a whole.

Pl. 14

NICOLAS POUSSIN

1594-1665

The Death of Hippolytus

Reverse: Another sketch in outline.

Pen and bistre, washed; 8⅞ x 13 in. (225 x 330 mm.)

PIERPONT MORGAN LIBRARY, New York, N. Y.

Collections: Marquis de Lagoy; Cavaceppi; Camuccini; Young-Ottley; Dimsdale; Sir Thomas Lawrence; Holford; Robinson; C. Fairfax Murray.

Bibliography: Catalogue of One Hundred Original Drawings . . . Collected by Sir Thomas Lawrence, Woodburn's Gallery, London, 1835, no. 83. C. Fairfax Murray, vol. I, p. 267, reproduced.

Exhibited: Buffalo, N. Y., Albright Art Gallery, 'Master Drawings,' 1935, no. 42. New London, Conn., Lyman Allyn Museum, 'Drawings,' 1936, no. 54. New York, Pierpont Morgan Library, 'World's Fair Exhibition,' 1939-40, no. 91; 1940, no. 109.

The serene and classic repose of Poussin's paintings is often lacking in his drawings. Although the nymphs and satyrs in his sketches for the *Bacchanals* (National Gallery, London) are full of frenzied and lustful abandon, translated onto canvas they become graceful participants in a rhythmic performance. 'La pensée préside à la naissance de chacun de ses tableaux,' says André Gide of Poussin; but if in his paintings he proclaimed the stoic philosophy he shared with Descartes, bringing order and discipline into the realm of feelings, he hardly exercised the same restraint when his pen or brush freely projected a vision or idea. Thus while no known painting corresponds to the drawing, *The Death of Hippolytus*, it is unlikely that Poussin would have allowed much of its torment and sweeping agony to carry over into a finished composition. The drawing tells the story of the young Athenian prince Hippolytus, who met his death in tragic fashion (Ovid, *Fasti:* III, 265). Dr. Walter Friedlaender suggests that the unusually dramatic treatment of the theme may be due to Poussin's acquaintance with a painting by Rubens of the same subject (engraved by Richard Earlom).

Pl. 15

NICOLAS POUSSIN

1594-1665

Holy Family

Pen and bistre, washed; 7¼ x 10 in. (184 x 253 mm.) *Date:* c.1648.

PIERPONT MORGAN LIBRARY, New York, N. Y.

Collections: Chantelou; Robinson; C. Fairfax Murray.

Bibliography: C. Fairfax Murray, vol. II, p. 71. Friedlaender, W., *The Drawings of Nicolas Poussin,* London, 1939, no. 46, pl. 30.

Exhibited: New York, Barnard College, Fine Arts Department, 1939. New York, Pierpont Morgan Library, 'World's Fair Exhibition,' 1939, no. 89.

In 1648 Poussin painted a *Madonna of the Steps* (Duke of Sutherland Collection), a variation on one of his favorite religious subjects. A preliminary sketch for this composition, the Morgan Library drawing, despite its weakness of execution, hints at the noble character of the painting. Against the background of columns broken by the horizontal intersection of steps the artist has placed a group of six figures. The scene achieves an effect of grandeur and repose, derived no less from the bearing of the figures than from the noble classic architecture of the setting. The studied arrangement of balanced units recalls Poussin's method of first making a pencil and bistre sketch of the proposed composition, then modeling the figures in wax, disposing them in appropriate attitudes, and finally dressing them in garments of colored paper or silk. So, too, the buildings and settings were constructed in wax and the figures inserted, with the proper light creating the transfigured appearance that he translated to canvas. Technically, this drawing is inferior to Poussin's best work and may possibly be a studio copy, but the artist's manner of silhouetting figures, his rapid notations for compositional detail, such as the fountain sketched lightly in the left foreground, are rendered convincingly.

Pl. 16

CLAUDE GELLÉE, called LE LORRAIN
1600-1682

View of the Tiber at Rome

Bistre, pen and wash drawing on white paper; 10½ x 8 in. (266 x 202 mm.)
Inscribed by a later hand, lower left: *Claudio Gelle.*

WILLIAM ROCKHILL NELSON GALLERY OF ART, Kansas City, Mo.

Bibliography: Tietze, H., *European Master Drawings . . .* , New York, 1947, no. 55, reproduced.

Exhibited: New London, Conn., Lyman Allyn Museum, 'Drawings,' 1936, no. 55.

Rome has been called the birthplace of romantic landscape. To the artists from the north who came to the fount of classicism, Rome was more than the relic of an antique world, for on the outskirts of the Eternal City they found the everchanging panorama of the Campagna, beside which their northern skies paled and their woodlands grew dim.

Steeping himself in the natural beauty of his adopted land, Claude never tired of watching the changing effects of sun and shadow upon the hills that surround the city. Fantastic silhouettes of trees, sheer cliffs and looming mountains evoke a mysterious grandeur whose spatial and atmospheric effects have their counterpart in the river landscapes that the Chinese artists of the Sung dynasty built up entirely in tones of monochrome wash.

Claudio Gille.

Pl. 17

CLAUDE GELLÉE

1600-1682

Landscape with Cattle

Reverse: Two pencil sketches of figures: *David Using a Sling; Goliath with a Spear Attacking Him.*
Pen and bistre wash and black chalk on cream laid paper; 10 x 15¾ in. (253 x 401 mm.)
Date: c.1640. Inscribed by a later hand, lower left: *Claudio Gellee.*

CLEVELAND MUSEUM OF ART, Cleveland, Ohio.

Collections: Sir Abraham Hume; Lord Alford; Earl of Brownlow.

Bibliography: Francis, H. S., 'A Landscape Drawing by Claude Lorrain,' *Bulletin of The Cleveland Museum of Art,* June 1928, pp. 127-9, frontispiece. *Master Drawings,* Albright Art Gallery, Buffalo, January 1935, no. 47, reproduced.

Exhibited: Buffalo, N. Y., Albright Art Gallery, 'Master Drawings,' 1935. New York, Durlacher Brothers, 'An Exhibition of Painting and Drawings by Claude Lorrain,' 1938, no. 11.

If Claude came to idealize nature in many of his studio drawings and paintings, his studies were nevertheless the outgrowth of many years of the closest observation of her moods and features. The German artist Sandrart describes frequent sketching tours with Claude in the romantic environs of the Campagna, where many of Claude's first impressions were recorded. Ruskin was to see little in them that pleased him: 'The evil landscape round Rome exhibits no pure and healthy nature, but a diseased and overgrown flora among half-developed volcanic rocks, loose calcareous concretions and mouldering wrecks of buildings . . .' But Ruskin is here overlooking Claude's supreme gift. A few strokes of the pen and warm touches of bistre, these swift studies are miracles of light transforming nature's aspects. Out of the very elements that Ruskin deprecated, Claude, in drawings like *Landscape with Cattle,* reconstructs his scenes, the happy massing of foliage set against a luminous sky, the wild hills, the dreamlike horizon inviting one's eye into unknown regions. The carefully balanced figures in the foreground are doubtless studio-drawn rather than a direct transcript. *The Skirts of the Woods,* dated 1640, in the British Museum (Hind, A. M., *The Drawings of Claude Lorrain,* London, 1925, plate 9) shows so similar a treatment as to suggest a like date for the Cleveland drawing. Other fine Claude drawings are in the Morgan Library and Robert Lehman Collection.

Pl. 18

JACQUES CALLOT

1592-1635

Landscape with Soldiers

Pen; 4½ x 7¼ in. (113 x 183 mm.)

CITY ART MUSEUM, St. Louis, Mo.

Collections: Mark Oliver; Durlacher Brothers.

Exhibited: New York, Durlacher Brothers, 'Old Master Drawings,' 1937, no. 35.

The bloody nationalist feuds and religious crusades between France, Spain, and the Netherlands—the Thirty Years War—served as the setting for Callot's tragic and violent pictorial dramas. Mercenary soldiers, swaggering lansquenets looting and firing towns, these are the dramatis personae of his 'Miseries of War.' But though Callot deplored the savagery and stupidity, his eye was nevertheless caught by the color and pageantry of the militia in action. In hundreds of sketches he recorded sorties, sieges, and manœuvers, setting down the patterns of opposing masses and lines with bravura effects. The extraordinary verve of his minuscule jabs of ink catch the prance and swagger of diminutive figures plying their lances and halberds with gusto. Callot is known to have been present at the Siege of Breda, where he made numerous sketches of military engagements. His sketch books of this period contain many sheets that resemble the *Landscape with Soldiers.*

Pl. 19

JACQUES CALLOT

1592-1635

Sketches of Ballet Dancers

Red crayon on white laid paper; 8¼ x 11¼ in. (210 x 285 mm.)

(Gift of Print and Drawing Club), THE ART INSTITUTE OF CHICAGO, Chicago, Ill.

Collections: Grosjean-Maupin.

Bibliography: Lieure, J., *Jacques Callot, La Vie artistique*, Paris, 1929, vol. I, pl. LXIX, fig. 153; vol. II, p. 28. Schniewind, C., 'Three French Drawings,' *Bulletin of The Art Institute of Chicago*, September-October 1942, vol. XXXVI, pp. 68-9, reproduced.

Exhibited: Chicago, The Art Institute of Chicago, 'Drawings Old and New,' 1946, no. 6.

Callot's sinuous line lent itself to the fugitive motion and grace of dancing. Fascinated by the theater and pantomime of every sort, he turned to the stage for those subjects that are now counted among his finest. During his stay in Florence he had occasion to witness the lavish theatrical entertainments, ballets, and pageants held at the Medici court, and to draw inspiration from the superb dancers. The figures in this drawing may have been preliminary notes for the etching, *Les Deux Pantalons* (Lieure, op. cit., no. 173), which appeared in 1616, while Callot was in Florence, or his *Balli di Sfessania* (Lieure, nos. 379-402), published in Paris about 1622.

Pl. 20

JACQUES BELLANGE

1594-1638

The Hunter Orion Carrying Diana on His Shoulders

Pen and bistre wash; 11 x 8 in. (279 x 202 mm.) Inscribed, lower left, in later hand: *Belange.*

JOHN S. THACHER, Washington, D.C.

Collections: Colnaghi.

The mannerism of Jacques Bellange of Nancy reaches back to the first School of Fontainebleau, but a more direct influence was that of the Italian mannerists Ventura Salimbeni, Federico Zuccaro, and Federico Barocci. Most of the paintings that Bellange is known to have executed for the palace of the dukes of Lorraine perished during the wars that devastated the duchy in the seventeenth century, but his remaining etchings and drawings show a brilliant handling of almost every graphic medium. The richest collection of his drawings is today in the Hermitage (12); the Ecole des Beaux Arts owns six sheets, the Louvre two, and the Albertina one. The Thacher drawing is the only known example of this artist's work in America. It is a free rendering of a drawing by Luca Penni (one of the Italian artists attached to the first Fontainebleau School), known from its engraving by Ghisi (reproduced, Pittaluga, M., *L'Incisione italiana ne cinquecento*, Milan, 1928, fig. 126). Bellange's engraving of the subject is described as 'the hunter Orion carrying Diana, the goddess of the forests, on his shoulders,' and bears the legend: *Gaudet amans nympha si raptor agenore nata* (Robert-Dumesnil, A.P.F., *Le Peintre-Graveur français*, vol. v, 1841, p. 94, no. 56). In its flowing line and bold use of wash, its bizarre gestures and surcharged animation the drawing of *Orion* displays a strong similarity to the figure in the right foreground of a *Pietà* by Bellange (reproduced, Kameskaia, T., 'Les Dessins de Jacques Bellange au Musée de l'Ermitage,' *Gazette des Beaux-Arts*, August 1929, pp. 72-8, fig. 1.)

Pl. 21

CLAUDE MELLAN
1598-1688

Portrait of Cardinal Richelieu

Pencil; 6 x 4⅝ in. (153 x 117 mm.) *Date*: c.1642.

(Edward B. Greene Collection), YALE UNIVERSITY ART GALLERY, New Haven, Conn.

Collections: Earl Spencer; Edward B. Greene.

Bibliography: Wolf, A., *The Edward B. Greene Collection of Engraved Portraits and Portrait Drawings* . . . , . . . New Haven, 1942, p. 138, no. 6, reproduced.

The drawing of Jean Armand du Plessis, Duke and Cardinal de Richelieu, chancellor of Louis XIII, is a replica of a pencil drawing in the National Museum, Stockholm (reproduced in Wengström, G., 'Claude Mellan: His Drawings and Engravings,' *Print Collector's Quarterly*, XI, 1924, p. 10 ff.). Claude Mellan, born in Picardy, went to Rome at the age of twenty-six and entered the studio of Vouet, whose paintings he engraved. On his return to Paris in 1642, he entered the service of Louis XIII as engraver, and became a resident of the Louvre. It was during this year that he did the pencil sketches that served as studies for the portrait of the Cardinal. Incisive in stroke and sensitively expressed, the drawing, done shortly before the Cardinal's death, exhibits the meticulous craftsmanship and psychological astuteness that were to establish Mellan's fame as the foremost engraver in France.

Pl. 22

EUSTACHE LE SUEUR
1617-1655

St. Bruno(?)

Black chalk heightened with white; buff paper; 13½ x 9⁵⁄₁₆ in. (342 x 236 mm.)

FOGG MUSEUM OF ART, Cambridge, Mass.

Collections: Sir Robert and Lady Witt.

Bibliography: Mongan and Sachs, vol. I, p. 313, no. 592; vol. III, fig. 301.

A student of Simon Vouet, who helped to foster a taste for the antique in France, Le Sueur acknowledged his master's influence for many years. Through Vouet and through contemporary Italian engravings, he also came under the spell of Raphael and Poussin, whose noble vision of antiquity is mirrored in many of Le Sueur's compositions. In 1645 he received a commission from the Carthusian monks for a series of paintings depicting the life of their founder, St. Bruno, to decorate the cloister arcades of the Chartreuse at Paris. Le Sueur told the story of the saint in twenty-nine scenes, each instinct with his own piety and gentle devotion. To narrate action while extolling solitude and contemplation was a challenging problem which he resolved by grouping figures in simple, harmonious relationships, concentrating on purity and expressiveness of line. There are many studies of single figures and component groups in the Life of St. Bruno series; this drawing with its lucidity and amplitude of design appears to be such a preliminary sketch.

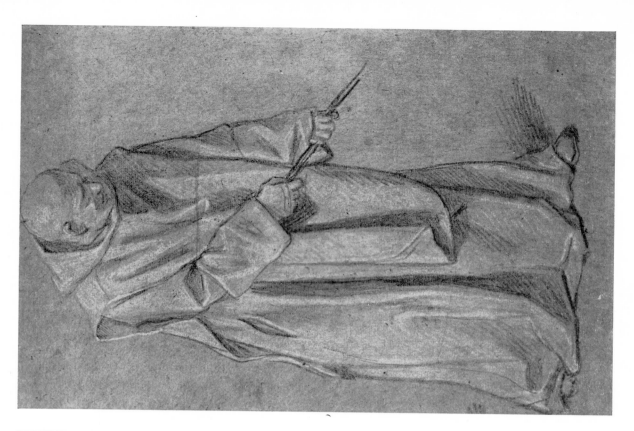

Pl. 23

NICOLAS DE LARGILLIÈRE

1656-1746

Portrait of a Young Boy

Black chalk on gray paper; 7⁹⁄₁₆ x 11³⁄₁₆ in. (191 x 282 mm.)

Mrs. C. I. Stralem, New York, N. Y.

Collections: Duke of Warwick; J. P. Heseltine.

Bibliography: Heseltine, no. 44, reproduced.

Exhibited: Buffalo, N. Y., Albright Art Gallery, 'Master Drawings,' 1935, no. 56. San Francisco, Golden Gate International Exposition, 'Master Drawings,' 1940, no. 63.

The half-length figure of a young boy (called *Louis the Dauphin* in the Warwick and Heseltine catalogues) combines French elegance and Flemish softness in the manner quite characteristic of Nicolas de Largillière. Having served his apprenticeship in Flanders, Largillière owed much to Rubens and even more to Peter Lely in whose London workshop he acquired the formula for fashionable portraiture done in a loose flowing style verging on the flamboyant. A prolific painter, he has left few drawings, so that attributions must be considered cautiously. The identity of the subject, too, is conjectural. The young boy is certainly not a dauphin, for the only heir to the crown whom Largillière could have painted as a six- or seven-year-old boy was the great-grandson of Louis XIV, afterwards Louis XV (born 1710, Dauphin 1712-15). Yet the costume indicates that the drawing was made before 1700; possibly around 1695; the style of the drawing too, with its insistence on elaborate detail, is of the transition period at the end of the seventeenth, rather than the beginning of the eighteenth century.

Who is the winsome lad, clearly of noble birth, whom the artist has shown in the costume of a courtier? He might be the son of James II of England, James Stuart, Prince of Wales, known in France as the 'Chevalier de St. Georges,' and to history as the Old Pretender. Born in 1688, this young Stuart prince came as an exile to the court of France, where he was brought up with the royal children. Largillière painted him with his sister Louisa as a boy of about seven, the approximate age of the child in this drawing. The painting (*Illustrated List of the Portraits in the National Portrait Gallery*, London, 1928, pl. xx) dates from about 1695, and while the drawing cannot be directly connected with it, it is of the same period and quite possibly portrays the same person. Mrs. Stralem also owns a drawing of the Duke of Burgundy by Largillière.

Pl. 24

HYACINTHE RIGAUD

1659-1743

Portrait of a Nobleman

Black and white chalk, pencil, wash, and Chinese white on blue-green paper, squared off for reproduction; 14¾ x 11⁵⁄₁₆ in. (374 x 287 mm.)

YALE UNIVERSITY ART GALLERY, New Haven, Conn.

Collections: Edward B. Greene.

Bibliography: Wolf, A., *The Edward B. Greene Collection of Engraved Portraits and Portrait Drawings . . .*, New Haven, 1942, no. 10, pp. 139-40, pl. XXXIV.

With the rise of French nationalism under Louis XIV, portraiture entered upon a phase of renewed popularity; artists were besieged with commissions for state portraits of the royal family and official likenesses of administrative personages and of the nobility. The seventeenth-century portrait, conceived as a psychological document done with parsimonious economy and austere Jansenist reserve, gave way to a contrasting fashion: florid faces and imposing countenances surmounted by elaborate powdered wigs, grandiose figures attired in full regalia, loom out of canvases. Hyacinthe Rigaud, Spanish-born painter who came to Paris in 1680, possessed a talent suited to such a program. Rarely wasting time on accessories, leaving to assistants like Charles Parrocel the battle-scene backgrounds of military portraits, while others supplied landscapes, draperies, floral and architectural settings, he concentrated on the portrait itself, posing his sitter in an attitude of authority and pomp as substitutes for character and purpose. However, he made meticulous records of the portions done by his own hand. Pose and costume are often repeated, as in the Yale University *Portrait of a Nobleman,* which duplicates the attire and attitude of the young Marquis Neri Corsini, whom Rigaud painted in 1688 (reproduced in Nugent, M., *All' Esposizione de Ritratto, Palazzo Vecchio,* Florence, 1912, p. 55). This procedure is accounted for by the frequent entries in Rigaud's notebook: 'habillement original' and 'habillement répété.' The indentity of the sitter in the Yale drawing is unknown; hence it is difficult to say for whom the costume was first designed. Done on squared paper, the drawing was doubtless a preparation for an engraving, though no such painting by Rigaud is known.

Pl. 25

ANTOINE WATTEAU

1684-1721

Head of Luigi Riccoboni

Red and black crayon; 5⅞ x 5⅛ in. (148 x 128 mm.) *Date:* c.1718.

METROPOLITAN MUSEUM OF ART, New York, N. Y.

Collections: Dumesnil; Miss James; Niel; Marquis de Biron.

Bibliography: Catalogue, Marquis de Biron Collection, Galerie Georges Petit, Paris, 1914, p. 67, no. 63, reproduced. Wehle, H. B., '*Le Mezzetin* by Antoine Watteau,' *Metropolitan Museum of Art Bulletin,* January 1935, pp. 12-18. Allen, J. L., 'Drawings from the Biron Collection,' *Metropolitan Museum of Art Bulletin,* March 1938, pp. 77-8, reproduced. Williams, H. W., Jr., 'Some French Drawings from the Biron Collection,' *The Art Quarterly,* vol. II, 1939, pp. 48-55, reproduced. Benisovich, M., 'The French Drawings of the Metropolitan Museum,' *Burlington Magazine,* March 1943, p. 70.

Exhibited: New York, Metropolitan Museum of Art, 1946.

The finest Watteau in the United States, *Le Mezzetin,* formerly owned by Catherine the Great, is now in the Metropolitan Museum. H. B. Wehle has identified the subject as Luigi Riccoboni, the Italian actor who appears also in the painting *Love in the Italian Theater* (Kaiser Friedrich Museum). Of greatest interest is this drawing from life, a preliminary study for *Le Mezzetin.*

The actors of the Italian *comedia dell'arte,* expelled by decree of Louis XIV for having offended his prudish mistress, Madame de Maintenon, were welcomed back joyfully after his death by the Regent Philip of Orléans. In May 1716 the troupe began its engagement in Paris, with Luigi Riccoboni as head of the company. The actor enjoyed great popularity in his favorite role of Mezzetin (the Italian Mezzetino, or half measure), an impudent rogue whose antics as valet and amorous adventurer the public applauded with delight. Watteau, who had always been an ardent admirer of the theater, has left us a vivid record of Riccoboni in the role of this stock character. Known to his generation as a painter of *fêtes galantes,* a chronicler of frivolous pastimes, Watteau reveals himself in this drawing as an artist of profound seriousness. His skill with his crayon, at once as delicate and incisive as that of the surgeon with his scalpel, exposes underlying character. Rarely has a more eloquent portrait been achieved with such modest means.

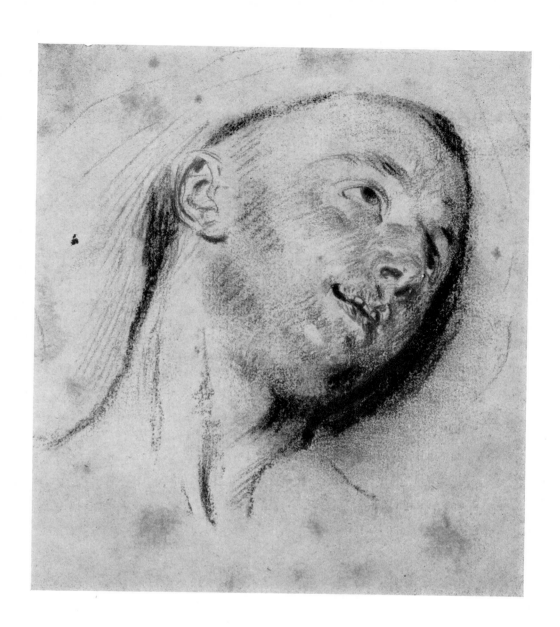

Pl. 26

ANTOINE WATTEAU

1684-1721

Half-length Figure of a Woman with Hands Folded

Red and black chalk; 10 x 5½ in. (253 x 140 mm.)

Forsyth Wickes, New York, N. Y.

Collections: Heseltine; David-Weill.

Bibliography: Heseltine, no. 78, reproduced. *David-Weill catalogue*, vol. III, p. 501, reproduced.

Exhibited: London, Grafton Galleries, 'National Loan Exhibition,' 1909-10, no. 53. San Francisco, Golden Gate International Exposition, 'Master Drawings,' 1940, no. 504. New York, Wildenstein Galleries, 'French Pastels and Drawings from Clouet to Degas,' 1944.

The reaction against the elaborate formality of court art under Louis XIV occurred during the last years of his reign, clearing the atmosphere for the intimate and revolutionary work of Watteau. It was in the vast reservoir of his sketch books that Watteau found the details closely observed, swiftly and accurately recorded, upon which he drew at random for his larger compositions. Thus the *Woman with Hands Folded* served, with certain variations, as a preliminary study for the figure of a woman holding a dog in the *Garden Party* (Dresden Museum). This simply posed figure, which achieves strength and solidity through its vigorous, unbroken linework and breadth of modeling, was engraved by Boucher in reverse in the *Figures de différents caractères* (Goncourt Catalogue, no. 614).

Pl. 27

ANTOINE WATTEAU
1684-1721

A Woman Seated

Red, black, and white chalk; 10 x 6¾ in. (260 x 171 mm.)

PIERPONT MORGAN LIBRARY, New York, N. Y.

Bibliography: Goncourt, E. de, *Catalogue raisonné d'Antoine Watteau*, 1875, no. 591; *Cent Dessins de Watteau gravés par Boucher*, 1892, no. 63.

Exhibited: New York, New York Public Library, 1919. Buffalo, N. Y., Albright Art Gallery, 'Master Drawings,' 1935, no. 58. Hartford, Wadsworth Atheneum, 1938. New York, Pierpont Morgan Library, 'World Fair Exhibition,' 1939, no. 95; 1940, no. 113, reproduced.

Watteau attained his pre-eminence as a draftsman by the virtuosity of his line and a dazzling use of the medium he made peculiarly his own—a combination of red and black chalk (*à deux crayons*), or red, black, and white chalk (*à trois crayons*). Often done on colored paper, these drawings have a sparkling freshness and vigor. The gracefully posed young woman recalls the *Figure du Printemps* in the Louvre (Marotte, L. and Dacier, E., *Watteau*, 1930, pl. I). It was doubtless the same model who posed for *La Servante de Watteau* (Nicolle, M., 'Watteau dans les Musées de Province,' *Revue de l'Art*, July 1921, p. 132). It is supposed that she was his servant, since no professional models posed in the nude in Watteau's time.

Pl. 28

ANTOINE WATTEAU
1684-1721

Sheet of Studies: *Standing Woman and Seated Child*

Red, black, and white chalk; 10 x 8½ in. (253 x 215 mm.) Collector's marks at lower right: William Esdaile, Lord Spencer.

Mrs. Henry Blum, New York, N. Y.

Collections: Hone; Lord Spencer; E. Coxe; W. Esdaile; Heseltine.

Bibliography: Heseltine, no. 91, reproduced.

Exhibited: London, Grafton Galleries, 'National Loan Exhibition,' 1909-10, no. 47.

Watteau was not all spontaneity and verve; a good deal of painstaking care went into the preparation of his working drawings, which, when incorporated into his paintings, lost none of their *élan*. More often, however, he simply filled his sketch books with figures from life, impressions grasped out of a multitude of human acts and gestures, and stored up for later reference. The study sheet of a standing woman and a seated child holding a compass was not used in any known composition by Watteau; yet the child's figure takes its place among the finest characterizations: the tousled hair, the diffident, slouching posture, the look of expectation and urgency as though some game had been interrupted, are here conveyed with the swift and simple lines of Watteau's crayon.

Pl. 29

ANTOINE WATTEAU

1684-1721

Sheet of Studies: *Heads of Women*

Red, black, and white chalk; 10 x 8½ in. (253 x 215 mm.)

FORSYTH WICKES, New York, N. Y.

Collections: Miss James; de Goncourt; Huquier; Groult.

Bibliography: Parker, K. T., 'The Drawings of Antoine Watteau, in the British Museum,' *Old Master Drawings*, June 1930, p. 27.

A counterproof of this study sheet is in the British Museum (reproduced, Uzanne, O., *Antoine Watteau*, pl. XXIV). During the eighteenth century chalk drawings were often reproduced in offset by dampening the sheet and pressing it against another sheet of paper. The offset is generally paler and more mechanical, though often it shows signs of having been retouched to approximate the tonal qualities of the original. The shading of the British Museum drawing is, of course, in reverse, and may have been made in preparation for an engraving of the Wickes study sheet.

Lancuw...

Pl. 30

ANTOINE WATTEAU

1684-1721

Sheet of Studies: *The Violinist*

Red and black chalk on grayish paper; 11½ x 9½ in. (291 x 241 mm.)

HOWARD STURGES, New York, N. Y.

Collections: Doucet.

Bibliography: Tourneux, M., 'La Collection Jacques Doucet,' *Les Arts*, December 1904, p. 4, reproduced. *Société de reproduction des dessins de maîtres*, 2ᵉ année, 1910, reproduced. Dacier, E., and Nicolle, M., *Collection Jacques Doucet*, Paris, 1912, pl. 64.

Studies of a Violinist is from the heart of Watteau's sketch-book work, one of the sights that attracted him as he wandered abroad at random, hastily noting down the passing scenes about him, the strolling actors and musicians who appear with such frequency in his paintings. His purpose, however, lies not in material for formally composed musical conversation pieces; his interest centers on the lives and ways of the musicians themselves. He sketches them offguard, practicing or tuning up, lost for the moment to the rest of the world and themselves in their absorption. Where Gillot renders the picturesque or genre aspect of the performers, Watteau searches out the psychological interaction between the performer and his art. His musicians are not merely engaged in producing melodic sounds, but are shown physically transformed, like Degas's ballet dancers in rehearsal, molded in the act of creating their art. The grace and charm of the violinist's stance are part of his poised attention to the tuning sounds. Watteau is similarly absorbed, equally concentrated as he sketches the player tuning up, for he is searching out the nicest balance between the angle of approach and the axis on which his image of the player is to be projected.

In the two studies Watteau sets down an alternate choice. In the upper view the violinist delicately adjusts the pegs while he plucks or thrums the strings, listening intently. In the other version, the body of the fiddler presents an accented twist; Watteau lowers the bow to horizontal in order to offset the sharper angle; but now the right hand is obscured while all the emphasis is on the left hand turning the peg ever so slightly. Yet Watteau's concern is clearly not with the hand alone, for he might have re-sketched it separately in the new position, but with the relation of the whole, the hands to the body and face at different angles; hence the repetition of the figure.

With the simplest of means and astonishing vivacity, Watteau has seized upon the interior life of his subject; in all the vitality of the moment and the intensity of the action, the violinist becomes the mirror of the artist Watteau, for he seeks with great delicacy of the hand and ear the perfect key and pitch, the exact turn of the peg, as Watteau, with similar hand and eye, seeks the choicest line and truest angle of vision.

Pl. 31

ANTOINE WATTEAU

1684-1721

Sheet of Studies: *Two Heads of Women*

Red, black, and white chalk; 5 x 7¼ in. (125 x 184 mm.)

Mrs. Henry Blum, New York, N. Y.

Collections: Heseltine.

Bibliography: Heseltine, no. 93, reproduced.

The romantic vision of an *Embarkation for Cytherea* called forth in Watteau those indefinable gifts for poetic phrasing and nuances of color harmony that captured and fixed forever the image born of a nostalgic yearning; but making on-the-spot sketches of the actors who were to take part in this lyrical tableau was another matter. In his studies from life, like the *Two Heads of Women*, Watteau becomes a documentary realist, sensitive to their graces but equally intent on conveying the roguish look and gesture, the bearing and attitude. The drawing was engraved by Boucher in the *Figures de différents caractères* as no. 41 (*Goncourt Catalogue*, no. 392). The head to the right is a study for the woman seated in the bark, in the *Embarkation for Cytherea* (Berlin version); it exists also in a single study in colored chalks at the Louvre.

Pl. 32

NICOLAS LANCRET

1690-1743

Studies for *Le Déjeuner au Jambon*

Red chalk; 7¼ x 9⅝ in. (183 x 243 mm.)

Mrs. C. I. Stralem, New York, N. Y.

Bibliography: Catalogue of Drawings of the French Eighteenth Century School, Walter Burns, Sotheby, Wilkinson & Co., London, 22 March, 1923, no. 8.

Exhibited: Buffalo, N. Y., Albright Art Gallery, 'Master Drawings,' 1935, no. 62. San Francisco, Golden Gate International Exposition, 'Master Drawings,' 1940, no. 63.

As a draftsman, Watteau's follower Lancret, who had been his fellow-student in Gillot's workshop, had far less originality and technical skill than Watteau, but considerable freshness and charm. The *Déjeuner au Jambon*, his most popular picture, was painted for Louis XV as one of four panels in a *petit cabinet* at the Versailles palace, and is typical of the lively and intimate style that made derisive sport of the Grand Manner. The sketch of two gourmands feasting, a study for the *Déjeuner au Jambon*, has a freedom and impulsiveness of line quite lost in the painting.

Pl. 33

HUBERT F. BOURGUIGNON, called GRAVELOT
1699-1773

Portrait Sketch of a Man

Red chalk; 10¾ x 7⅝ in. (274 x 193 mm.)

Cooper Union Museum for the Arts of Decoration, New York, N. Y.

Collections: Erskine Hewitt.

The rise of the modern novel in eighteenth-century France and England opened a new field for the draftsman and engraver. Among the first to utilize contemporary manners rather than allegory in pictorial interpretations of these novels was Gravelot. During a long sojourn in England, where he won the friendship of Garrick and high praise from Walpole, Gravelot provided vignettes and drawings for many books, among them *Pamela* and *Tom Jones.* Many of his drawings were engraved and published, singly or in series, on both sides of the Channel. The *Portrait Sketch of a Man* falls into this category, for it is mentioned by the Goncourts as having been engraved in London by Mayor. (Goncourt, E. and J. de, *L'Art du dix-huitième siècle*, 3rd ed., Paris, 1882, p. 38, *Gentilhomme assis de profil sur un banc de pierre, une main appuyée sur le bec d'une canne*). Gravelot's thin and elegant line, adapted to the engraver's tool, defined with ease the crisp satins and brocades, dainty lace, and flowing wigs of eighteenth-century society.

Pl. 34

FRANÇOIS BOUCHER

1703-1770

Study for *Aurora and Cephalus*

Red chalk heightened with white; 14⅝ x 9⅛ in. (370 x 231 mm.)

Date: 1733. Inscribed, lower left: *ƒ. boucher*.

HONORABLE IRWIN LAUGHLIN, Washington, D.C.

Collections: Peter Jones; Greene; Basil Dighton.

The figures that dissolve in the shimmering atmosphere of Watteau's pantomimes spring to full-bodied life in the canvases of Boucher, whose search for beauty in the human form was ceaseless and passionate. First and foremost a decorator, Boucher yielded to the concept of the nude as a unit in an ornamental scheme, but his complete acceptance of the classical ideal also taught him to respect the dignity and anatomic integrity of the human body. The study for the central figure in *Aurora and Cephalus* (Nancy Museum) retains a feeling of bodily weight and substance, balanced by—almost subordinate to—the pulsating rhythm and supple flow of line. The resilient contours, the warm shading, the luminous sheen produced by Chinese white, heighten the sense of palpable form and living structure, elements that carry their own function in the design. Boucher was to return to this composition some thirty years later when he painted another version of the *Aurora and Cephalus* legend (the Louvre), and again when he illustrated this episode for the luxurious edition of Ovid's *Metamorphoses* (1767). Sketches for these later versions exist in the National Gallery of Art (Widener Collection) and in the Laughlin Collection.

Pl. 35

FRANÇOIS BOUCHER

1703-1770

Study for *The Judgment of Paris*

Charcoal on gray paper; 13¾ x 7½ in. (349 x 190 mm.) *Date: c.*1754. Inscribed: *f. Boucher.*

(Gift of James D. Phelan), CALIFORNIA PALACE OF THE LEGION OF HONOR, San Francisco, Calif.

Collections: James D. Phelan.

In 1754 Boucher painted a series of four mythological subjects that became part of the *décor* of a boudoir in the Hôtel de l'Arsenal, one of the residences of Madame de Pompadour. At the height of his creative power, he turned once more to classical mythology, interpreting four scenes from the loves of Venus—*The Visit of Venus to Vulcan; Cupid a Captive; Venus and Mars Surprised by Vulcan;* and *The Judgment of Paris.* These panels, now in the Wallace Collection, were supposedly commissioned by the Marquise for Louis XV; after his death they were ordered removed by Louis XVI, who thought them immoral. They proclaim Boucher's inventive mind, his imaginative use of the classical vocabulary, his innate feeling for graceful decorative design, his revolutionary treatment of space—the underlying motive in rococo art —and above all, his mastery of form. The drawing of a female nude is a study for the figure of Minerva in the *Judgment of Paris.* Unmistakably from life, it is a structural analysis of the human body in action. One feels the artist searching for the rhythmic line to convey motion, for the right volume to express form. Such linear potency is rarely found in Boucher's early drawings, never in his later ones. The figure of Minerva shows him at his mature best. The Goddess of Wisdom, whose charms were spurned in favor of the Goddess of Love, is seen proudly and disdainfully floating off into the Olympian realm. Her arched body, in its forward and upward movement, is made to suggest, with admirable perception, the hidden energy released by an emotional drive.

F. Boucher

Pl. 36

FRANÇOIS BOUCHER

1703-1770

Study for *Venus and Mars Surprised by Vulcan*

Black and red chalk, heightened with white chalk; 8⅝ x 15½ in. (218 x 393 mm.) *Date*: 1754.

Honorable Irwin Laughlin, Washington, D.C.

Collections: Peter Jones; Greene; Basil Dighton.

Exhibited: London, Burlington Fine Arts Club, 'Drawings by Deceased Masters,' 1917, no. 87.
London, Burlington House, 'French Art, 1200-1900,' 1932, no. 766.

This superb study from life became the central figure in one of the four panels that Boucher painted for Madame de Pompadour's Hôtel de l'Arsenal, in 1754, his *Venus and Mars Surprised by Vulcan*, now in the Wallace Collection. A finished study of the same figure (Maurice Fenaille Collection) allows further insight into the artist's working methods—his careful study of the human figure from life, followed by the gradual evolution of his esthetic formula, utilizing the female nude as a unit in a decorative ensemble.

Pl. 37

FRANÇOIS BOUCHER
1703-1770

Two Nudes: Study for *Pan and Syrinx*

Charcoal and white chalk; 15½ x 10 in. (392 x 253 mm.) *Date: c.*1759. Inscribed: *f. Boucher.*

(Estate of Mrs. W. H. Crocker), SAN FRANCISCO MUSEUM, San Francisco, Calif.

Collections: Mrs. W. H. Crocker.

In 1759 Boucher painted the *Pan and Syrinx* now in the National Gallery, London. Pursued by Pan, the Nymph Syrinx seeks refuge in the river Ladon and is changed into a reed from which Pan fashions his syrinx or flute. In the present drawing, a study for the *Pan and Syrinx* (cf. *National Gallery Illustrations, Continental Schools*, London, 1937, p. 28), Boucher has used Ovid's version, according to which Syrinx fled into the arms of a sister nymph (*Metamorphoses*, I, 689-712). A related drawing, both in subject and execution, is the *Two Water Nymphs*, in the Morgan Library (cf. C. F. Murray, III, 103). Both drawings are done in charcoal and white chalk, a medium that Boucher greatly favored for his figure studies, particularly the sketches from life.

Pl. 38

FRANÇOIS BOUCHER

1703-1770

Tête-à-Tête

Black chalk heightened with white; 13⅛ x 9⅛ in. (333 x 231 mm.) *Date:* 1764. Inscribed: *F. Boucher* 1764.

(Widener Collection), NATIONAL GALLERY OF ART, Washington, D.C.

Collections: Stainville; Chalandray; Cypierre; Joseph E. Widener.

Bibliography: Comstock, H., 'Master Drawings in San Francisco,' *Connoisseur*, September 1940, pp. 114-15.

Exhibited: New London, Conn., Lyman Allyn Museum, 'Drawings,' 1936, no. 95. San Francisco, Golden Gate International Exposition, 'Master Drawings,' 1940, no. 7.

'The rich,' wrote a contemporary of Boucher, in commenting on his pastoral scenes, 'would not be pleased to gaze upon the grossness and suffering of our peasants; for it might recall the misery of which they themselves were perhaps the cause . . .' And while a gaily beribboned shepherd at the Opéra Comique serenaded his shepherdess:

> *La rose est moins fraîche*
> *Un beau jour moins serein . . .*
> *C'est la fleur de la pêche*
> *Qui colore son teint . . .*

Voltaire complained sarcastically, 'Why all these shepherds! Nothing but shepherds everywhere!'

The eighteenth century loved reason and logic but it adored pleasure and refinement; Boucher's pastorals corresponded exactly to these tastes. His bucolic idylls are set in landscapes that might easily serve as backdrops for an *opéra comique*—a profusion of flowers and shrubs, trees with festooned branches surrounding antique fountains and thatched cottages. Here shepherds and their companions disport themselves, twining garlands of flowers and exchanging vows of love. Never wearying of this theme, Boucher produced scores of pastoral subjects throughout the 'fifties and 'sixties. His favorite models are a dainty little shepherdess and a shepherd lad with dark curly hair, often attended by a playful brown and white spaniel. We meet them in *La Musette* (the Louvre), which he painted in 1753, and again in *The Cage* (the Louvre), done ten years later. They have not aged, nor have their rustic surroundings changed. In the drawing *Tête-à-Tête* (engraved by Demarteau under the title of *Conversation galante*) they are once again engaged in amorous play, among the customary rustic surroundings. Although this late drawing is not without a certain charm, it lacks the precision and vitality of line that distinguish Boucher's early and his mature work.

Pl. 39

MAURICE QUENTIN DE LA TOUR

1704-1788

Self-Portrait

Gouache on vellum; 14½ x 11¼ in. (367 x 285 mm.)

MRS. ALBERT BLUM, New York, N.Y.

Collections: Count de Robiano.

Bibliography: Sale Catalogue, *Dessins Anciens, Collection Cte. de Robiano*, Frederik Muller, Amsterdam, 1926, no. 463, reproduced.

'They think that I only seize upon their features,' wrote Maurice Quentin de la Tour of his clients, 'but without their knowing it, I reach down into their very depths and grasp them in their entirety.' (Leroy, A., *La Tour*, Paris, 1933.) Not only the pastel portraits of his sitters—men of affairs, of talent and intellect, actresses and reigning beauties of the day—but his numerous self-portraits reveal this constant probing into mood and character, this striving to plumb the depths and capture the hidden self. In this study for one of his self-portraits, probably that known from the contemporary engraving by Schmidt (Besnard, A., *La Tour*, Paris, 1928, frontispiece), a few strokes of the brush have selected out of the mass of obscuring detail those tell-tale lines that sum up the essence of the man.

Pl. 40

LOUIS CARROGIS, called DE CARMONTELLE

1717-1806

Dauberval and Mademoiselle Allard in the Pas de Deux Mimé

Pen, gouache, and watercolor; 13⅞ x 11¾ in. (352 x 298 mm.)

JOHN S. THACHER, Washington, D.C.

Bibliography: The Dance Index, vol. VI, no. 3, March 1947, reproduced on cover.

The career of Louis Carrogis, who adopted the surname de Carmontelle, is paralleled by that of many brilliant figures in the eighteenth century, including Voltaire. Of humble origin, he became reader to the Duc de Chartres, and master of ceremonies at the innumerable lavish *fêtes* held at the court of the Duc d'Orléans. A spirited writer and composer of talent, Carmontelle also painted the sets for more than forty comic operas and comedies that he wrote and produced privately for his noble patrons; the hundreds of portraits he drew of those who frequented the court circles—nobles and wealthy merchants, men of letters, musicians, scientists, and soldiers—he considered a mere pastime, a sort of album of his age, which he compiled for his own amusement. Many of his subjects were of topical interest, but he has also set down with a naive grace and a lively sense of curiosity such incidents as the musical performance of the child prodigy, Mozart, and the ballet *Sylvie* (1766), danced by Dauberval and Mademoiselle Allard, who scored a spectacular triumph in their day.

Pl. 41

GABRIEL DE SAINT-AUBIN

1724-1780

Irruption de Chanteurs Costumés

Watercolor heightened with gouache; 9 x 11¼ in. (228 x 286 mm.)
Inscribed, in center scroll upheld by two figures: *G.S.*

MRS. HERBERT N. STRAUS, New York, N.Y.

Collections: Perignon; Destailleur; Lion; Marthe Brandes; G. Seligman.

Bibliography: Catalogue, A. Perignon Collection Sale, Paris, 1864, no. 462, reproduced. *Catalogue, H. Destailleur Collection Sale,* Paris, 1896, no. 869, reproduced. Dacier, E., *Gabriel de Saint-Aubin,* Paris, 1931, vol. II, no. 659, pl. XXIV (as *Divertissement théatral donné au cours d'une soirée*). Royal Academy, *Catalogue, French Art,* no. 758, reproduced.

Exhibited: London, Burlington House, 'French Art, 1200-1900,' 1932, no. 758. Buffalo, N.Y., Albright Art Gallery, 'Master Drawings,' 1935, no. 77. New York, Jacques Seligman, 'The Stage,' 1939, no. 6.

In Gabriel de Saint-Aubin the eighteenth century had its most intimate and untiring chronicler. Hundreds of his sketches, often dashed off at great speed, afford us the most minute documentation of court and city life. This frail and lonely man covered every aspect of his locale, setting down in feverish strokes street scenes, salon gatherings, theatrical performances, public merrymakings—the volatile, debonair life around him. His free-flowing line moving effortlessly across the sheet, and his atmospheric effects, anticipating the Impressionists, are not readily apparent in this highly finished composition. But the lively use of gouache, accentuating structure and movement, captures the gay and impromptu character of the entertainment—a group of costumed musicians bursting into a room where a dazzling company is assembled.

Pl. 42

GABRIEL DE SAINT-AUBIN

1724-1780

Portrait of a Clockmaker

Watercolor heightened with gouache; 9 x 5¼ in. (228 x 132 mm.)

FORSYTH WICKES, New York, N. Y.

Collections: Fourquevaux; Comte de la Béraudière; Beurdeley; David-Weill.

Bibliography: Goncourt, E. de, *L'Art du dix-huitième siècle*, Paris, 1875, vol. I, p. 428. Dacier, E., 'La Collection David-Weill,' *Société de reproduction des dessins de maîtres*, 1913, reproduced. *L'Amour de l'Art*, January 1925, p. 12, reproduced. *David-Weill*, vol. III, p. 183, reproduced.

Exhibited: Paris, Hotel Charpentier, 'Exposition des Saint-Aubin,' 1925, no. 94.

The restlessness that obsessed Gabriel de Saint-Aubin and drove him from the salons and concert-halls into the teeming streets of Paris fills his drawings with pulsating life, animating even so static a composition as this portrait of a clockmaker. The swirling figurines, the circular clocks, the movement of the arm, all unite to convey the feeling of motion, the mechanism of the clock, and the flux of time. Although he was a master of graphic expression, Gabriel de Saint-Aubin handled gouache with uncommon dexterity; in the *Portrait of a Clockmaker* this element of color plays an important part in producing a dramatic effect.

Pl. 43

JEAN PILLEMENT

1726-1808

Decorative Design for a Title Page

Black chalk; 12⁹⁄₁₆ x 8⁹⁄₁₆ in. (318 x 217 mm.) Inscribed: *jean Pillement.*

Cooper Union Museum for the Arts of Decoration, New York, N.Y.

Collections: Decloux.

Exhibited: New London, Conn., Lyman Allyn Museum, 'Drawings,' 1936, no. 98.

Pillement's gift for decorative design found a natural outlet in the fanciful *chinoiseries* and *bergeries,* the stock-in-trade of the Gobelins and Beauvais tapestry works. Since the days of Louis XIV the Royal House had shown a partiality for the elaborate refinement of Ming ceramics and textiles; and catering to this taste, Boucher, Le Prince, and Pillement invented endless variations on the Chinese motifs found in these precious objects. Though he had never been to China, Pillement's oriental idylls gained for him a reputation as one of the finest painters of *chinoiseries,* and eventually Marie Antoinette appointed him court painter. The *Design for a Title Page* of a book on Chinese parasols is an attractive example of Pillement's rich and graceful fancy. His red chalk drawings and delicately tinted watercolor, done with rococo exuberance, typify the exquisite artificiality of the day.

Jean Pillement

Jean Pillement · Titre d'un cahier de parasols chinois.

Pl. 44

JEAN BAPTISTE GREUZE

1725-1805

Sketch for a Composition

Pen, sepia, and gray wash; 12½ x 19¹¹⁄₁₆ in. (316 x 499 mm.) Inscribed, lower left: *Greuze fecit.*

MRS. HERBERT N. STRAUS, New York, N.Y.

Bibliography: Tietze, H., *European Master Drawings* . . . , New York, 1947, no. 106.

While Boucher and Fragonard created their sparkling world of disporting nymphs and shepherdesses for a perfumed aristocracy, Greuze turned to the moral counsels of Diderot and Rousseau; 'Rendre la vertu aimable et le vice odieux.' Following this cue, he turned to the middle classes and the peasantry for themes of homely virtue rendered in sentimental anecdotes. This sketch shows the quality of his drawing, particularly in pen and ink, when he discards the restrictions of academic formulas. His pen swirls across the sheet creating movement and rhythm, while he depends on strong washes to secure the solid planes and spatial effects.

Pl. 45

JEAN HONORÉ FRAGONARD

1732-1806

Sketch for *The Sacrifice of Coresus*

Black chalk washed with sepia; 13¾ x 18⅛ in. (347 x 461 mm.) *Date: c.1764.*

PIERPONT MORGAN LIBRARY, New York, N.Y.

Collections: C. Fairfax Murray.

Bibliography: C. Fairfax Murray, vol. I, p. 288.

In 1765 Fragonard exhibited in the Salon the picture that had gained him membership in the Academy, an elaborate composition entitled *Le grand prêtre Coresus se sacrifie pour sauver Callirhoe* (Louvre). So popular was the painting that it was bought for the Gobelins works, to be woven into a tapestry. But Fragonard, kept waiting for his money for eight years, was obliged to turn to *sujets galants* in order to earn his livelihood. In the study for *Coresus* in the Morgan Library, one senses the complete assurance of an artist who has mastered his style and is able to compose for bravura effects. The dramatic disposition of the figures and the strong chiaroscuro effects recall Fragonard's debt to Tiepolo, but the vapory atmospheric effects and the treatment of space are in the best vein of rococo art.

Pl. 46

JEAN HONORÉ FRAGONARD
1732-1806

Villa Boncompagni-Ludovisi

Pencil and gray wash; 8⅞ x 13⅞ in. (235 x 350 mm.)

PHILIP HOFER, Cambridge, Mass.

Exhibited: Worcester, Mass., Worcester Art Museum, 'Inaugural Exhibition,' 1933. Buffalo, N. Y., Albright Art Gallery, 'Master Drawings,' 1935, no. 81.

An early drawing, done during Fragonard's first visit to Italy, the *Villa Boncompagni-Ludovisi* aims principally at an architectonic rather than atmospheric effect. The building is drawn meticulously with pencil, while gray washes are used to bring out the full effect of the structure as well as the landscape in the foreground. The artist's later impressionistic landscapes are already foreshadowed, however, in the broken contours of hills and the suggestion of shrubbery.

The Villa Boncompagni-Ludovisi, now destroyed, was built in the seventeenth century by Cardinal Ludovico Ludovisi, and later passed into the hands of the wealthy merchant family of Boncompagni-Ludovisi.

The Fragonard drawings that have reached American collections include some of his most poetic landscape studies, such as *Pines of the Villa Doria Pamphili* (Robert Lehman), *Gardens of the Villa d'Este* (Estate of Mrs. W. H. Crocker), and *Fête à Rambouillet* (Mrs. Herbert N. Straus).

Pl. 47

JEAN HONORÉ FRAGONARD
1732-1806

Scene in a Park

Pen, brush, sepia, and black ink; 7⅝ x 9⅞ in. (193 x 250 mm.) Inscribed: *Frago.*

CLEVELAND MUSEUM OF ART, Cleveland, Ohio.

Collections: Walferdin; Marquis de Turenne; Comte Arthur de Vogue.

Bibliography: Hourticq, L., *Le Paysage français de Poussin à Corot* . . . Paris, 1925, p. 63. Sizer, T., 'Drawings by Boucher and Fragonard,' *Cleveland Museum Bulletin*, vol. XIII, 1926, pp. 5-8, reproduced.

Exhibited: Paris, Petit Palais, 'Exposition du Paysage français de Poussin à Corot,' 1925, no. 440.

Though he was only fifteen when he left his native Provence, the memory of its luxuriant natural surroundings stayed with Fragonard all his life. Later in Italy, he was to be overawed by the spectacle of magnificent ruins lending nature everywhere an air of subdued sadness. How gratefully must he have surveyed once again the smiling landscape of southern France, which invited his eye to dwell on the abundant foliage against which figures move vivaciously. The impressionistic *Scene in a Park* has all the lightness and joyous sparkle of a sketch that does not seek to mirror all of nature's charms, but merely suggests them with careless assurance.

Pl. 48

JEAN HONORÉ FRAGONARD

1732-1806

The Firecrackers

Pen and bistre wash over pencil on cream paper; 10⅜ x 15 in. (262 x 380 mm.) *Date: c.*1765.

MUSEUM OF FINE ARTS, Boston, Mass.

Collections: Varanchon de Saint-Geniès; Morel-Vindé; de la Lottière; Templier; Des-Closières; David-Weill.

Bibliography: Goncourt, E. de, *L'Art du dix-huitième siècle*, Paris, 1895, vol. 3, p. 274. Portalis, R. de, *Honoré Fragonard . . .*, Paris, 1889, p. 194. Doucet, G., *Peintres et graveurs libertins du* XVIIIᵉ *siècle*, Paris, 1913, pp. 47-8. 'Honoré Fragonard,' *Dessins de maîtres français*, VI, Paris, 1927, pl. 43, reproduced. Wilenski, R. H., *French Painting*, Boston, 1931, p. 164. Robiquet, J., *La Femme dans la peinture française*, Paris, 1938, p. 122, reproduced. Mitchell, A. A., 'A Drawing by Fragonard,' *Bulletin of the Museum of Fine Arts*, Boston, June 1945, pp. 20-22.

Exhibited: New York, Wildenstein Galleries, 'French XVIII Century Pastels, Water Colors and Drawings from the David-Weill Collection,' 1938.

During the 1760's, while Boucher's career was drawing to a close, his former student-assistant Fragonard returned to Paris after an extended period of study and travel in Italy to become almost at once a favorite painter of *sujets galants*. For Boucher's mythological romances and lyrical pastorals he substituted piquant scenes of contemporary *moeurs*; the amours of Olympus and the Elysian fields gave way to those of the boudoir, the hayloft, and the scullery. The drawing of *Les Pétards* (*The Firecrackers*), an amusing spectacle of three girls startled out of sleep by a bunch of exploding firecrackers let down through a trap door in the ceiling, suggests the sprightly humor with which Fragonard titillated his contemporaries. Done about 1765, *Les Pétards*, like its companion piece, *Les Jets d'eau*, was engraved by Pierre-Laurent Auvray, and became one of the most popular *estampes galantes* of the eighteenth century.

Pl. 49

JEAN HONORÉ FRAGONARD

1732-1806

Concert in a Drawing Room

Bistre wash; 9 x 7 in. (228 x 178 mm.)

CHARLES E. DUNLAP, New York, N. Y.

Collections: Serullaz; David-Weill.

bliography: David-Weill, vol. III, p. 113, reproduced.

The animation of a musical performance with both participants and spectators grouped in graceful attitudes was a favorite theme of polite genre with eighteenth-century artists. Fragonard was often at his best in depicting such anecdotal scenes as *Concert in a Drawing Room*. By an imaginative use of wash he suggests the setting of a spacious room, peopled with the familiar salon figures, elegantly costumed. The young girl seated at the clavichord, the lady playfully teasing a little dog, the gesturing gentleman, the couple turning the pages of a book, how casually they participate in this intimate scene! Here Fragonard's art indeed 'conceals its technique while displaying its facility.'

Pl. 50

JEAN HONORÉ FRAGONARD

1732-1806

The Letter

Wash over pencil on white paper; 15¹¹⁄₁₆ x 11⅜ in. (398 x 289 mm.)

(Gift of Tiffany and Margaret Blake), THE ART INSTITUTE OF CHICAGO, Chicago, Ill.

Collections: Lebrun; Duc de Montesquiou-Fezensac; David-Weill.

Bibliography: Portalis, R. de, *Honoré Fragonard . . .*, Paris, 1889, pp. 300-304. Dacier, E., 'La Collection David-Weill,' *Société de reproduction des dessins de maîtres*, 1913, 5ᵉ année, reproduced. *Renaissance de l'art français*, July 1921, p. 359, reproduced. 'Honoré Fragonard,' *Dessins de maîtres français*, VI, Paris 1927, pl. 39. *David-Weill*, vol. III, p. 117, reproduced. Royal Academy, *Catalogue, French Art*, no. 687, pl. 174. *The Art Quarterly*, Winter 1946, pp. 77-8, reproduced. *Bulletin of the Art Institute of Chicago*, March 1946, pp. 26-7. Schniewind, C.O., *Drawings Old and New*, The Art Institute of Chicago, 1946, pp. 13-14. Tietze, H., *European Master Drawings . . .*, New York, 1947, pl. 102.

Exhibited: Paris, Pavillon Marsan, 'Exposition d'Oeuvres de J.-H. Fragonard,' 1921, no. 126. London, Burlington House, 'French Art, 1200-1900,' 1932, no. 808. New York, Wildenstein Galleries, 'David-Weill Collection,' 1938.

Preserved for many years in a portfolio of drawings owned by the Duc de Montesquiou-Fezensac, *The Letter*, (also called *The Surprise* or *Spanish Conversation*) has not become faded in appearance, as have so many of Fragonard's wash drawings, but remains fresh and sparkling today, one of the finest examples from that master's hand. As in *La Liseuse* in the Louvre (Nolhac, *Fragonard*, 1906, p. 94), *La Confidence* (*Prestel Gesellschaft* XIV, pl. 18), and *La Rêveuse* (Forsyth Wickes Collection), drawings stylistically related to *The Letter*, Fragonard has recorded a fleeting incident, suspending action in time, so that movement and gesture are simultaneously caught and reflected.

Pl. 51

JEAN HONORÉ FRAGONARD

1732-1806

Portrait of a Neapolitan Girl

Sepia wash; 13⅝ x 10¾ in. (345 x 273 mm.) Inscribed, lower right: *Naples, 1774 Femme de Ste Lucia.*

Mrs. C. I. Stralem, New York, N. Y.

Collections: Marmontel; Hodgkins; Seligman.

Bibliography: Sale Catalogue, Marmontel Collection, Paris, March 28, 1898, no. 24.

Exhibited: Paris, Pavillon Marsan, 'Exposition . . . Fragonard,' 1921, no. 173 (as *Jeune Italienne*).

The portrait of this handsome peasant girl in her finery was done during Fragonard's second trip to Italy, where he had gone in 1773 as a guest of his friend and patron, Bergeret de Grancourt. This was the artist's most mature period; his reputation was made, but some of his best work still lay ahead of him. If he was more often impelled to gratify patrons with gay and decorative or frivolous canvases, Fragonard could readily escape, in studies like this, to seriousness and directness. Here he relies less on the virtuosity of his brushwork than on the directness of his vision to point up the qualities of strength and peasant wholesomeness.

Pl. 52

JEAN HONORÉ FRAGONARD

1732-1806

Rinaldo, Astride Baiardo, Flies off in Pursuit of Angelica

Illustration for Ariosto's *Orlando Furioso*

Pencil, wash, and ink; 10$\frac{5}{16}$ x 15$\frac{1}{8}$ in. (261 x 383 mm.) *Date: c.* 1795.

(Rosenwald Collection), NATIONAL GALLERY OF ART, Washington, D.C.

Collections: Walferdin; Roederer; Rosenbach.

Bibliography: Selections from the Rosenwald Collection, National Gallery of Art, Washington, 1943. Mongan, E., Hofer, P., and Seznec, J., *Fragonard Drawings for Ariosto,* New York, 1945. Kennedy, R. W., 'Fragonard Drawings for Ariosto,' *Art in America,* July 1946, vol. 34, pp. 163-4, 'Fragonard Drawings for Ariosto,' *Burlington Magazine,* July 1946, vol. 88, p. 180.

Exhibited: Washington, D.C., Phillips Memorial Gallery, 'Drawings by Fragonard,' 1945. Northampton, Mass., Smith College Museum of Art, 'Exhibition of the Illustrations to the Poems of Ariosto and Tasso,' 1946.

The eighteenth-century artists were distinguished illustrators, and many classics owed their popularity to the visual interpretation that artists like Fragonard gave to their characters. In 1795 he completed a set of 136 drawings for a special edition of *Orlando Furioso*. The project itself was never realized. Today most of the drawings are in American collections.

Diderot complained that Fragonard's drawings 'were like masses of cotton wool, lacking body and precision, apt to vanish into smoke.' Rinaldo galloping away on the fabulous horse Bayardo looks indeed like some vaporous essence about to vanish into space.

Pl. 53

HUBERT ROBERT

1733-1808

Sketch of an Imaginary Roman Building

Pen and sepia wash; 17½ x 12½ in. (445 x 317 mm.) *Date:* 1770. Inscribed, with false signature: *Frago.*

THE CLEVELAND MUSEUM OF ART, Cleveland, Ohio.

Collections: Baron D. Vivant-Denon.

Bibliography: Baron D. Vivant-Denon Sales Catalogue, no. 736 (as Fragonard). Sizer, T., 'A Drawing by Hubert Robert,' *Cleveland Museum of Art Bulletin,* November 1927, pp. 143-4, reproduced.

Exhibited: Buffalo, N. Y., Albright Art Gallery, 'Master Drawings,' 1935, no. 87.

___

When Hubert Robert came to Rome in 1754, the recently revived interest in classical antiquity and archaeological exploration had mounted to fever pitch. A few years earlier, Piranesi's *Views of Rome* and *Opere Varie* had appeared, revealing in a series of plates etched and engraved with superlative skill the stately monuments and noble ruins amid the picturesque settings of Rome. Piranesi's prints and the paintings of Pannini fed the nostalgia for the antique, which the young Frenchman had brought with him. He entered the studio of Pannini and there learned the repertory of forms, which on his return to France served him as an inexhaustible storehouse of themes and compositions and earned him the title *Robert des Ruines.*

The sketch of what apears to be a great staircase in a Roman bath is an imaginary scene. By a subtle use of sepia washes, the composition gains depth and tone, while crisp strokes of the pen accentuate the structural elements. The figures, modeled in wash and outlined in pen, provide a lively contrast to the massiveness of the architecture.

Pl. 54

HUBERT ROBERT

1733-1808

The See-Saw

Ink and watercolor; 17¼ x 12¾ in. (436 x 323 mm.) Inscribed, at right: *Robert.*

CHARLES E. DUNLAP, New York, N. Y.

Collections: Gilbert Levy.

___

Together with Fragonard, Hubert Robert was commissioned by the Abbé de Saint-Non, archaeologist and art patron, to make pictorial records of the most beautiful sites and monuments in Italy, which were to serve as illustrations for the Abbé's ambitious publication *Voyage pittoresque en Italie.* For the Abbé, this great venture resulted in bankruptcy, but for both Fragonard and Robert the Italian assignment yielded a wealth of pictorial themes.

To Hubert Robert, the sight of urchins or country people disporting themselves among the noble ruins of Italy was not an uncommon one. The artist's fancy delighted in the genre scenes set against an architectural background of the past— women washing clothes, children playing blindman's-buff or see-saw. The broken column tottering in the foreground, the majestic buildings of Rome seen in the distance, and the Farnese *Hercules* provide the incongruous setting for two youngsters balancing on the see-saw. Their game is a lively note of discord, which breaks the spell of melancholy and decay that broods over the scene. A broken tombstone in the foreground bears the Latin inscription *Qui se exaltat humiliatur et qui se humiliat exaltaritur,* which sets forth the moral: 'He who exalts himself shall be humbled and he who humbles himself shall be exalted.'

The artist's interest in the current vogue for antiquity compels him to use many stereotyped 'props,' but his facility in the use of washes to create atmospheric effects breathes freshness and life into the ruins.

Pl. 55

AUGUSTIN DE SAINT-AUBIN

1736-1807

Studies of a Girl

Pencil, slight touches of red crayon; 8⅛ x 6½ in. (207 x 165 mm.) *Date: c.*1792.

ART INSTITUTE OF CHICAGO, Chicago, Ill.

Collections: Baron Pichon; Baron Jerome; J. P. Heseltine.

Bibliography: Drawings of the French School from the Collection of J. P. Heseltine, London, 1911, no. 30, reproduced. Schniewind, C., 'Three French Drawings,' *Bulletin of the Art Institute of Chicago,* September-October 1942, vol. XXXVI, pp. 68-9, reproduced.

Exhibited: Chicago, Art Institute of Chicago, 'Drawings Old and New,' 1946, no. 48, pl. VII.

An accomplished draftsman as well as a superb engraver, Augustin de Saint-Aubin was one of the great book illustrators of the eighteenth century, engraving not only his own work but the illustrations of contemporaries such as Boucher and Gravelot for such notable publications as the 1757 *Decameron.* If he considered his own age 'à travers une lorgnette de marquis,' delighting in such courtly scenes as *Le Concert* and *Le Bal paré,* his most famous engravings, his drawings have the free and impulsive quality, the suppleness and spontaneity of line that do not recur until the mid-nineteenth century, with Daumier, Degas, and Toulouse-Lautrec.

The rapid notation of lines seeking an informal, almost casual, effect of figures hastily glimpsed in a variety of poses and immediately set down is strikingly 'modern' in its approach and utilizes a technique that was later fully exploited by Degas and Toulouse-Lautrec. The figure of the girl (at the top, left), emptying a vessel, was used in an engraving in color by Antoine S. Philippeaux and Jean-Baptiste Moret, entitled *La Jardinière* (Bocher, E., *Saint-Aubin Catalogue,* Paris, 1879, no. 416).

Pl. 56

JEAN-MICHEL MOREAU (le Jeune)
1741-1814

Perfect Harmony

Pen and bistre and bistre wash; 10⅛ x 8⅝ in. (256 x 219 mm.)
Inscribed and dated, lower left: *J. M. Moreau Lejeune* 1776.

HONORABLE IRWIN LAUGHLIN, Washington, D.C.

Collections: King Ludwig II of Bavaria (?); Guillaume de Rothschild; Goldschmidt-Rothschild.

Bibliography: Goncourt, E. de, *L'Art du dix-huitième siècle*, Paris, 1874, vol. 2, p. 177. Bocher E., *Les Gravures françaises du* XVIIIe *siècle, Jean Michel Moreau le Jeune*, Paris, 1882, no. 1355. Lawrence, H.W., and Dighton, B.L., *Les plus belles gravures françaises du dix-huitième siècle, en taille douce*, Paris, 1912, no. 226. Cohen, G., and Ricci, S. de, *Guide de l'amateur de livre à gravures du* XVIIIe *siècle*, VI, Paris, 1912, p. 359. von Carolsfeld, L.S., and Huth, A., *Die Sammlung Erich von Goldschmidt-Rothschild*, Berlin, 1931, p. 28, pl. 14. Royal Academy, *Catalogue, French Art*, p. 153, no. 714, reproduced. *Widener Collection of French Engravings*, London, 1923, vol. 4, p. 529.

Exhibited: London, Burlington House, 'French Art, 1200-1900,' 1932, no. 847.

'A harp, the favorite musical instrument with ladies of quality, emits harmonious sounds even if indifferently played, and enhances the charm of singing, nay of mere warbling.' The lady whose attention is divided between the music she makes and the words that are whispered into her ear is one of the fashionable *grandes dames* whose doings are recorded in the *Monument du costume* (1777), the most notable collection of engravings done in the eighteenth century. These appeared in three series of twelve plates each, the first after Freudeberg, the second and third after Moreau le Jeune. Intended as a record of *moeurs* in elegant circles during the last quarter of the eighteenth century, the engravings achieved enormous popularity both in France and abroad. Often verging on the *grivois*, these scenes of aristocratic genre titillated the public, and the collection, with text by an unknown author, proved to be one of the best sellers of the time. An accomplished draftsman, Moreau le Jeune became the pictorial raconteur of these gay episodes. *Perfect Harmony* was made for the engraving Number 20 in the second series. Other original drawings for several engravings in the *Monument du costume* are in the Laughlin collection; a single study of great charm is in the National Gallery, Widener Collection.

Pl. 57—58

JEAN-MICHEL MOREAU (le Jeune)

1741-1814

Portrait of Françoise, the Artist's Daughter

Pen and Chinese ink, washed; one of two pendants, each 3⅞ x 5¾ in.
(100 x 145 mm.) Goncourt stamp in lower-right corner.

FORSYTH WICKES, New York, N. Y.

Collections: Goncourt; Walter Burns; Mortimer Schiff.

Bibliography: Goncourt, E. de, *l'Art du dix-huitième siècle*, 3rd ed., Paris, 1882, vol. II, p. 189, reproduced.

The most worldly and sophisticated artists of the eighteenth century were often *âmes sensibles*— despite the artificial sentimentality affected by the leisure class, who demanded simpering pastorals, and despite the smug sentimentality of the *bourgeoisie*, who insisted upon moral precepts in art. Moreau le Jeune, like Chardin, Boucher, and Watteau, succumbed to the appeal of childhood; the portrait of his little girl Françoise, like Boucher's charming sketches of his own children, has a quality of secret delight, of winsomeness touched with pathos, that imparts a warm, pervasive feeling of intimacy to this little sketch. Two similar sheets, showing the artist's young daughter asleep, were in the Marius Paulme sale.

Pl. 59

JACQUES-LOUIS DAVID

1748-1825

Study for *The Oath of the Tennis Court*

Watercolor; 9 x 13½ in. (229 x 343 mm.) *Date:* 1790-91.

(Winthrop Bequest), FOGG MUSEUM OF ART, Cambridge, Mass.

Collections: Grenville L. Winthrop.

In 1790 David was asked to execute a painting commemorating the occasion of the Tennis Court Oath, sworn, on 20 July 1789, by the representatives of the Third Estate, who pledged themselves to give France a constitution. David accepted the commission enthusiastically, and in a series of preparatory sketches, unmistakably from life, portrayed the agitated groups of deputies, arms upflung, gesticulating in the wild tumult of the historic moment. The drawing reproduced has little that is studied or calculated; this is an eyewitness account by an artist who has been trained to convey the movement of surging crowds by means of quick strokes of the brush and touches of wash. Here David belongs to the eighteenth century, for he draws, as Mr. Sterling observes, in the spontaneous and spirited manner of Saint-Aubin (pl. 55) and other *dessinateurs* of the old régime. (*cf.* Sterling, C., *The Art of the French Revolution*, Wildenstein, New York 1943.)

This first conception, a study in mass psychology rather than a memorial tableau, was abandoned by the artist in favor of a later sepia sketch of a group of nude men in heroic attitudes (exhibited in the Salon of 1791 and now in the Louvre). In the realistic portrayal of their countenances, David continues to pay homage to the deputies, but the frenzied moment that he earlier captured has now been frozen into a sort of classic pantomime. It is in the early Fogg Museum drawing that the drama and spiritual significance of the occasion are to be seen. This is one of a group of sketches, seven of which are in the Winthrop collection, others being at Versailles and in the hands of Wildenstein and Company. David's projected work was never completed, for by the time it had reached an advanced stage, most of the members of the assembly whom he had so carefully portrayed had become suspect and were under the shadow of the guillotine.

Pl. 62

JEAN-AUGUSTE-DOMINIQUE INGRES

1780-1867

Lady and Boy

Pencil; 9⅜ x 7¼ in. (237 x 184 mm.) Inscribed, on front:
Ingres rome/1808; on back: *pour ma fille/Sirviere.*

(H. O. Havemeyer Collection), METROPOLITAN MUSEUM OF ART, New York, N.Y.

Collections: H. O. Havemeyer.

Bibliography: Catalogue, Havemeyer Collection Exhibition, Metropolitan Museum, 1930, p. 26, no. 181. Wilenski, R. H., *French Painting,* Boston, 1931, pl. 82. Rewald, J. 'Ingres and the Camera,' *Art News,* vol. XLII, no. 6, May 1943, p. 10. *Ingres: 24 Drawings,* New York, 1947, no. 9, reproduced.

Exhibited: Springfield, Mass., Springfield Museum of Art, 1939, no. 38. New York, Knoedler Galleries, 'David and Ingres,' 1940, no. 38.

The Villa Medici, where the French Academy in Rome was housed, serves as the background for the *Lady and Boy,* which Ingres has drawn with implacable accuracy of line and extraordinary ability to suggest the exact volume of each form. The lady, whose identity is unknown, appears singly in a drawing at the Fogg Museum of Art.

Pl. 63

JEAN-AUGUSTE-DOMINIQUE INGRES
1780-1867

Portrait of Leclère and Provost

Lead pencil on creamy white paper; 12⅜ x 9⅝ in. (314 x 243 mm.)
Inscribed, lower right: *Ingres D vit a Rome* 1812.

Smith College Museum of Art, Northampton, Mass.

Bibliography: Lapauze, H., *Ingres*, Paris, 1911, pp. 124, 128. *Art News*, 11 December, 1937, p. 17. *Smith College Museum of Art Bulletin*, June 1938, pp. 7-11, reproduced. *Burlington Magazine*, July 1939, pp. 3-13. *Parnassus*, December 1939, p. 40, reproduced. *Art News*, 6 January, 1940, p. 17, reproduced. *Art in America*, April 1940, p. 84.

Exhibited: Cleveland, Ohio, Cleveland Museum of Art, 1927. Springfield, Mass., Springfield Museum of Fine Arts, 1939. New York, Knoedler Galleries, 'David and Ingres,' 1940, no. 46.

In 1806 Ingres left for Rome to take up his studies at the French Academy, as the holder of the Prix de Rome, which he had won five years earlier. While he was there (1806-20) he earned his livelihood chiefly by making portrait drawings, for which he is said to have received no more than 40 francs each. Hundreds of these have survived, the greater portion being preserved at the Musée Bonnat, Bayonne, and the Louvre, while some threescore magnificent examples are in America. Aside from the evidence of mere industry, their number demonstrates a sustained level of abstract linear purity that is unequaled in the nineteenth century save for the production of Degas. It is a line, as David suggested, that possesses the exquisite delicacy and sinuous grace of Chinese drawings. The *Portrait of Leclère and Provost* is created within a rhythmic flow of lines whose resilience, with unerring precision and clarity of statement, preserves the supple flow of the living figures. It is for these qualities that Degas and Seurat looked to Ingres as their master.

Pl. 64

JEAN-AUGUSTE-DOMINIQUE INGRES

1780-1867

The Guillon-Lethière Family

Pencil; 10¾ x 8½ in. (272 x 215 mm.) Inscribed lower
left: *Ingres a/Monsieur Lethiere/ Rome* 1815.

THE MUSEUM OF FINE ARTS, Boston, Mass.

Collections: Guillon-Lethière; Bestegui.

Bibliography: 'A Drawing by Ingres,' *Bulletin of the Museum of Fine Arts*, Boston, June 1926, pp. 38, 39,
reproduced (cover). *The Arts*, February 1930, vol. 16, p. 382, reproduced. *Magazine of Art*,
November 1937, p. 11, reproduced. Pach, W., *Ingres*, New York, 1939, p. 102, reproduced.
Shoolman, R., and Slatkin, C. E., *The Enjoyment of Art in America*, Philadelphia, 1942,
pl. 507. Tietze, H., *European Master Drawings* . . . , New York, 1947, no. 124, reproduced.

Exhibited: Cambridge, Mass., Fogg Museum of Art, 'French Drawings and Prints of the Nineteenth Cen-
tury,' 1934, no. 43. Buffalo, N. Y., Albright Art Gallery, 'Master Drawings,' 1935, no. 94.
Philadelphia, Pennsylvania Museum of Art, 'Problems in Portraiture,' 1937. Washington, D.C.,
Phillips Memorial Gallery, 1938.

The family here portrayed is that of the son of Guil-
lon-Lethière, Director of the French Academy at
Rome. There is a study for the single figure of Guil-
lon-Lethière *fils* in the Musée Bonnat at Bayonne.
A study of his wife and child is in the Metropolitan
Museum of Art.

Pl. 65

JEAN-AUGUSTE-DOMINIQUE INGRES

1780-1867

Studies for *The Martyrdom of St. Symphorien*

Obverse: Man on horse, holding a staff, and other studies. Reverse: Nude man holding a chair aloft. Pencil on cream paper; 21¼ x 16 in. (539 x 406 mm.) *Date:* between 1826 and 1834.

WILLIAM ROCKHILL NELSON GALLERY OF ART, Kansas City, Mo.

Bibliography: Lapauze, H., *Ingres*, Paris, 1911, pp. 304-10. *Ingres: 24 Drawings.* New York, 1947, reproduced.

Exhibited: Springfield, Mass., Springfield Museum of Fine Arts, 1939. New York, Knoedler Galleries, 'David and Ingres,' 1940, no. 41.

In 1824 the State commissioned Ingres to do a painting for the Cathedral of Autun. The bishop of Autun requested a *Martyrdom of St. Symphorien*, a young Roman noble who had embraced Christianity. The episode was to be portrayed against the setting of Roman monuments at Autun, the prelate specifying the minutest details to be included in the composition. Ingres visited Autun in 1826, to gain first-hand knowledge of the background. There followed eight years of groping, during which the final version gradually emerged after repeated trial and error. Hundreds of preliminary sketches preserved at Montauban and elsewhere are an impressive record of the artist's untiring quest for the final realization of his theme. In the present drawings, the man holding a staff is a tentative study not used in the finished picture, while the two figures on the right became two of the principal actors—the centurion with outstretched arm, and the mounted soldier who gazes up at the young saint's mother. A smaller replica of the painting at Autun is in the Philadelphia Museum (Johnson Collection), while other preliminary sketches are at the Fogg Museum of Art in Cambridge.

Pl. 66

JEAN-AUGUSTE-DOMINIQUE INGRES

1780-1867

Study for the *Portrait of Madame d'Haussonville*

Pencil on white paper squared for enlargement; 9¼ x 11⅝ in. (234 x 294 mm.)
*Date: c.*1842-6. Inscribed, lower left: *Ing.*

(Paul J. Sachs Collection), Fogg Museum of Art, Cambridge, Mass.

Collections: Beurdeley; Wildenstein; Sachs.

Bibliography: Beurdeley Sale Catalogue, Galerie Georges Petit, Paris, 1920, no. 242.
Mongan and Sachs, vol. i, pp. 379-80; vol. iii, no. 704, fig. 375.

Exhibited: Petrograd, 'Exposition centennale de l'art français,' 1912, no. 664. Cambridge, Mass., Fogg Museum of Art, 'French Painting of the Nineteenth and Twentieth Centuries,' 1929, no. 86. St. Louis, Mo., City Art Museum, 1932. Brooklyn, N. Y., Brooklyn Museum, 1939.

It is curious that Ingres, whose primary fame rests on his portraiture, should have hated portrait painting. It was with the greatest reluctance that he accepted a portrait commission, and on occasion the sitter (the Baronness Rothschild, for example) would have to lay siege to the artist's studio before he consented to undertake the task. The results were almost invariably admirable, and, as in the case of the *Portrait of Madame d'Haussonville,* enchanted everyone, including Ingres.

The *Portrait of Madame d'Haussonville,* the young granddaughter of Madame de Staël, in the Frick Collection, has been called the most famous Ingres in America. It is easy to see why the artist, after a number of trial studies, of which this drawing is one, was pleased with the final result, though he felt that he had 'not done justice to all the graces of this charming model.' The sleek and sinuous line that he employs is admirably suited to the feminine graces of his subject. Delacroix called Ingres 'a Chinese artist lost in Greece,' while George Moore found hints of the Japanese masters in his work. There is indeed something of the swaying Oriental rhythm in his composition, a gift for creating patterns that is traditionally found more often in the East.

Pl. 67

JEAN-AUGUSTE-DOMINIQUE INGRES
1780-1867

The Family of Lucien Bonaparte

Pencil on white paper; 15¾ x 20½ in. (400 x 520 mm.) Inscribed
and dated, lower right: *J. Ingres, Del. Rome* 1815.

(Grenville L. Winthrop Collection), FOGG MUSEUM OF ART, Cambridge, Mass.

Collections: Charles Lucien Bonaparte; Charlotte Bonaparte Primoli; Count Joseph Napoleon Primoli;
Gluckstad; Gorm Rasmussin; Jacques Seligman; Grenville L. Winthrop.

Bibliography: Lapauze, H., *Ingres*, Paris, 1911, p. 180. *Ingres: 24 Drawings*,
New York, 1947, no. 10.

Ingres's talent as a portraitist was at the disposal of French residents and English tourists, artists and musicians, and the well-to-do Roman bourgeoisie. As his reputation grew, his clientele became more distinguished, including many members of the Imperial household. The family of Lucien Bonaparte, the Emperor's brother, posed during the 'hundred days' (20 March—28 June 1815), when Lucien had returned to France to aid his brother. Although the various members are not highly individualized—a strong family resemblance in part accounts for this—their figures are rendered with a grace of line that finds its analogy in the vibrant flow of music.

Pl. 68

JEAN-AUGUSTE-DOMINIQUE INGRES

1780-1867

Two Nudes: Study for *The Golden Age*

Pencil on white paper; 15⅜ x 11⁵⁄₁₆ in. (390 x 281 mm.) *Date:* 1843-8. Inscribed, lower left: *Ingres;* at the right in Ingres's handwriting: *cuisses un peu longues.*

(Grenville L. Winthrop Collection), FOGG MUSEUM OF ART, Cambridge, Mass.

Collections: Haro; Winthrop.

Bibliography: Ingres: 24 Drawings. New York, 1947, no. 20, reproduced.

'I can tell you that no man was ever more obsessed and enslaved by his thoughts than I. Night and day this obsession continues, for I do not just paint during the daytime—I execute what my thoughts have clarified during the night. Constantly a figure, a group, haunts me like a ghost, saying, "Make me like this, make me like that . . ." and all this is most exhausting.' Thus Ingres described to his friend Marcotte the genesis of his mural *L'Age d'Or.* (Delaborde, H., *Ingres,* Paris, 1870, p. 194)

He had received the commission for this painting during his second stay in Italy, where he directed the French Academy at Rome. In 1843, two years after his return to Paris, he responded to the invitation of the Duc de Luynes to come to Dampierre and there to decorate one of the galleries of the chateau. With characteristic zeal and thoroughness Ingres made some five hundred preparatory studies of single groups and figures to be used in this idyllic vision of the Golden Age, drawing upon classical lore, upon the enchanted visions of Watteau and upon his own imagination, which revelled in Arcadian dreams. No one, not even the Duc de Luynes, was allowed to see the mural until it was completed, but the response to this pagan ensemble was not altogether favorable, and Ingres abandoned the plan for a companion picture, *L'Age de Fer.*

The group in the Fogg Museum drawing does not appear in the final composition, but the female figure is repeated in a single study in the Musée Ingres at Montauban.

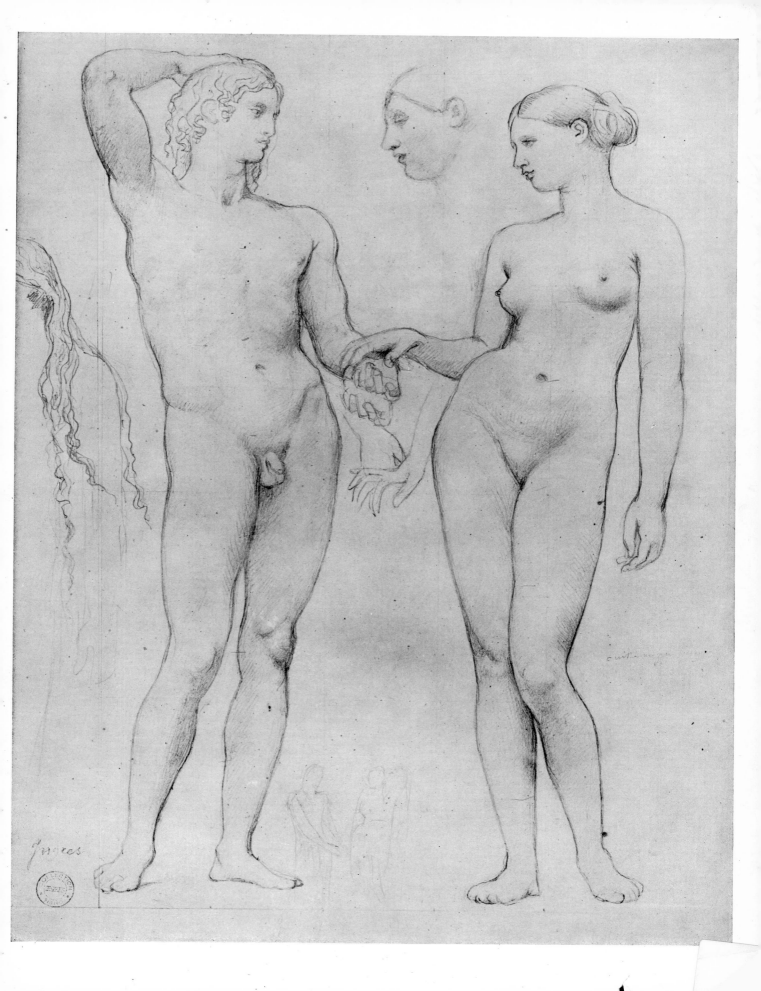

Pl. 69

JEAN LOUIS ANDRÉ THÉODORE GÉRICAULT

1791-1824

Frightened Horse

Pen and ink and sepia wash on gray paper; 9 x 10½ in. (228 x 266 mm.) Inscribed, lower right: *Géricault.*

DETROIT INSTITUTE OF ARTS, Detroit, Mich.

Collections: J. Peoli.

Bibliography: Berger, K., *Géricault Drawings and Watercolors*, New York, 1946, no. 4, reproduced.

Exhibited: San Francisco, California Palace of the Legion of Honor, 'Nineteenth-Century French Drawings,' 1947, no. 24.

Géricault's fancy for horses dated from his earliest youth, when he often stole away for happy hours at a local stable. It was natural that as a young man he should become a passionate devotee of those magnificent equestrian spectacles at the Cirque Olympique. Later, addressing himself to the study of old masters, he found the most responsive chord in his own temperament was struck by the elements of surcharged action in dramatic compositions. Thus his first Salon picture, *Officier de Chasseurs à cheval,* done at the age of twenty-one and borrowed from an engraving of Raphael's *Battle of Constantine,* already reflects his preoccupation with the portrayal of strenuous flexing of limbs and the interplay of muscular masses. Visiting England in 1821, he watched the Derby at Epsom Downs, and the sight of those handsome thoroughbreds, as well as the colored sporting prints and animal studies of Ward and Landseer, which were everywhere to be seen, confirmed Géricault once and for all in his preference for subject matter. It was to take on new meaning and value with the advent of Romantic doctrines three years later. The frightened animal in the Detroit sketch is a masterpiece of calligraphic drama, constructed of frenzied swirls and daubs of ink that barely contain the compressed power and untamed vitality here unleashed in a moment of fear.

Pl. 70

JEAN LOUIS ANDRÉ THÉODORE GÉRICAULT

1791-1824

Two Horses Cavorting

Reverse: Drawing of a man on horseback.
Pencil; 16⅛ x 20¾₁₆ in. (410 x 511 mm.)

(Gift of Robert Allerton), THE ART INSTITUTE OF CHICAGO, Chicago, Ill.

Collections: P. J. Chenavard; A. P. Roll; Duc de Trévise.

Bibliography: Delteil, L., 'Théodore Géricault,' *Peintre-graveur illustré*, Paris, 1924, vol. XVIII, no. 12. *Gros, Géricault, Delacroix*, Knoedler and Co., New York, 1938, no. 37. *Gros, Géricault, Delacroix*, The Art Institute of Chicago, Chicago, 1938-9, no. 37. Berger, K., *Géricault*, New York, 1946, no. 9, reproduced.

Exhibited: New York, Knoedler Galleries, 'Gros, Géricault, Delacroix,' 1938, no. 37. Chicago, The Art Institute of Chicago, 'Gros, Géricault, Delacroix,' 1938-9, no. 37. San Francisco, San Francisco Museum of Art, 'French Romantic Artists,' 1939, no. 37. Chicago, The Art Institute of Chicago, 'Drawings Old and New,' 1946, no. 23.

The early part of the nineteenth century has been called 'the golden age of lithography,' reflecting in its prints 'all the variety, impassioned spirit and new perception of the pictorial in the arts.' Géricault found this medium a happy one for translating some of his best graphic compositions; a lithograph dated 1818 entitled *Chevaux pommelés se battant dans une écurie* (Delteil 12) is a free rendering of a subject he was often to resume with many variations—horses in combat. The horse at the left in the Chicago drawing resembles very closely, as Schniewind points out, one of the horses in the 1818 lithograph. As Ingres in the endless search for perfection came to transmute the contour lines of the nude figure into an abstract beauty of their own, wherein the forms acquire a life and meaning wholly apart from their representational function, so Géricault in *Two Horses Cavorting* has refined the quality of his descriptive line, rhythmic and musical in its phrasing, giving it a pulsating and independent life.

Pl. 71

JEAN LOUIS ANDRÉ THÉODORE GÉRICAULT

1791-1824

Study for *The Riderless Horse Race*

Pen and ink; 7½ x 9¾ in. (190 x 247 mm.) *Date*: 1817.

WILLIAM ROCKHILL NELSON GALLERY OF ART, Kansas City, Mo.

Collections: M. H. Michel-Levy; Duc de Trévise.

Exhibited: Paris, Galerie Charpentier, 'Exposition Géricault,' 1924, no. 108. Rouen, Musée de Rouen, 'Exposition Géricault,' 1924. Paris, Maison Victor Hugo, 'La Jeunesse des Romantiques,' 1927, no. 1292. Paris, Galerie Bernheim Jeune, 'Géricault,' 1937, no. 110.

It was in Rome that Géricault witnessed a spectacle that held the very greatest interest for him: the riderless horse race, annually run at Carnival time. The feral beasts, rearing and plunging, held in check by peasant boys heedless of their very lives, were quickly seized upon by Géricault as the perfect Romantic subject, the pure example of unbridled passion and explosive energy tearing loose in wild movement. These free and untamed spirits Géricault sketched again and again, toward a projected painting whose heroic dimensions were to carry the stunning impact of the dynamic theme itself. Every phase and movement of this episode were essayed in a series of sketches ranging from summary notations, with the pen outlining form in a single stroke, to carefully finished details. But as the work progressed, Géricault's conception changed from one of realistic interpretation of men and horses in brutal conflict, to a classical frieze of monumental rhythms, with men and animals, stripped of individual traits, engaged in epic combat. In the study of a nude man he has singled out the figure in the foreground struggling with the horse, building it into a pyramidal composition of tremendous force. An unbroken line defines the contours of the rearing animal, while the nude figure with a few sparing strokes of the pen is rendered in all its massive and sculptural vigor. In this drawing, as in the more complete study at the Fogg Museum, Géricault, enormously aroused, yet conscious of classical traditions, has submitted the spontaneous and surcharged action to the discipline of formal design.

Pl. 72

JEAN LOUIS ANDRÉ THÉODORE GÉRICAULT

1791-1824

A Negro Soldier Holding a Lance

Brush and sepia and gray wash over pencil; 13¾₁₆ x 9¹³⁄₁₆ in. (335 x 249 mm.)

FOGG MUSEUM OF ART, Cambridge, Mass.

Collections: De L'Aage; Marmontel; Beurdeley; Paul J. Sachs.

Bibliography: Apollo, St. Petersburg, 1912, p. 23, reproduced. *Catalogue of the Beurdeley Collection Sale*, Galerie Georges Petit, Paris, 1920, pt. v, no. 167, reproduced. Clement, C., *Géricault*, Paris, 1879, pp. 443-4, no. 175 *bis*. Leporini, H., *Die Künstlerzeichnung*, Berlin, 1928, pl. 127. *Société de reproduction des dessins de maîtres*, pt. IV, Paris, 1912, pl. IV. Berger, K., IV, *Géricault Drawings and Watercolors*, New York, 1946, no. 46, reproduced.

Exhibited: Paris, 'Exposition centennale de 1900,' no. 984. St. Petersburg, Russia, 'Exposition centennale de l'art français,' 1912, no. 276. Geneva, 'Exposition centennale de l'art français,' 1918. Northampton, Mass., Smith College Museum of Art, 'Géricault,' 1929, no. 15. Cambridge, Mass., Fogg Museum of Art, 'French Painting of the Nineteenth and Twentieth Centuries,' 1929, no. 77. London, Burlington House, 'French Art, 1200-1900,' 1932, no. 900. St. Louis, Mo., City Art Museum, 1932. Brooklyn, N. Y., Brooklyn Art Museum, 1939. Washington, D.C., Phillips Memorial Gallery, 1940. Detroit, Mich., Detroit Institute of Arts, 1941. San Francisco, California Palace of the Legion of Honor, 'Nineteenth-Century French Drawings,' 1947, no. 25.

Aside from the appeal of the subject as singularly appropriate to Romantic doctrine, with its sympathy for the oppressed and the tyrannized, the superb physique of Joseph, the model, attracted Géricault as a challenge that called forth every talent for vigorous delineation and authoritative rendering of massed volumes.

Pl. 73

FERDINAND VICTOR EUGÈNE DELACROIX

1798-1863

Faust and Mephistopheles in the Students' Cellar-Tavern

Chinese ink and sepia wash; 10 x 8 in. (253 x 202 mm.) *Date: c.*1826. Stamp of the Delacroix Sale in lower-right corner.

PHILIP HOFER COLLECTION, Cambridge, Mass.

Collections: M. A. Pontremoli.

Bibliography: Delteil, L., *Le Peintre-Graveur Illustré,* Paris, 1906-30, vol. III, no. 64.

'M. Delacroix is a man of great talent who has found in Faust his proper nourishment. The French censure his wildness, but it suits him well here. He will, I hope, go through all Faust and I anticipate a special pleasure from the witches' kitchen and the scenes on the Brocken.' Thus Goethe commented on the lithographs that Delacroix had done for his immortal tragedy (Eckermann, *Conversations with Goethe*). The drawing of Faust and Mephistopheles carousing in the students' cellar, done in preparation for the lithograph (Delteil, 64), embodies all the elements of Romantic painting: strangeness and terror as the students become aware of their sinister visitor and his magic powers, swagger and bravado in their attitudes, action suspended at a dramatic moment, an atmosphere of mystery and exoticism enveloping the scene. Delacroix builds up his forms in washes of varying density, relying on a strong chiaroscuro for relief. A few details show linear accents—reckless, flying curves, and hasty scribbles that are the antithesis of Ingres's careful and delicate pencilwork, so disliked by Delacroix.

Pl. 74

FERDINAND VICTOR EUGÈNE DELACROIX

1798-1863

Armored Figure on Horseback

Pencil and sepia washes; 10¾ x 14¾ in. (272 x 398 mm.) *Date: c.*1828.

THE CLEVELAND MUSEUM OF ART, Cleveland, Ohio.

Exhibited: San Francisco, California Palace of Legion of Honor, 'Nineteenth-Century French Drawings,' 1947, no. 29.

The spell that the Middle Ages cast over nineteenth-century Europe accounts for a great deal of historical genre. Delacroix's *Bataille de Nancy*, a commission from the Minister of the Interior for the Museum of the City of Nancy, was to represent the defeat of Charles the Bold, Duke of Burgundy, a victory for the Duchy of Lorraine. Before undertaking the painting, Delacroix made a number of sketches of the combatants in the battle piece, concentrating particularly upon Charles the Bold, one of the last great figures of the Middle Ages. The drawing of an *Armored Figure on Horseback* is clearly related to other sketches of the same subject (cf. Escholier, R., *Delacroix, Etude pour Charles Le Téméraire,* pp. 233-94). It is instructive to note the artist's care in depicting armor; while in England, he and Bonington made a careful study of armor from specimens in a private collection. With its free use of washes in the construction of planes, broken and jagged to suggest the play of dramatic lighting, the approach is Impressionistic in all but name and stems from the example of Constable's *Hay Wain* (exhibited in the Salon of 1824), which had led Delacroix to repaint his *Massacre of Scio.*

Pl. 75

FERDINAND VICTOR EUGÈNE DELACROIX

1798-1863

Study for *The Execution of the Doge Marino Faliero*

Watercolor; 9⅛ x 6⅞ in. (232 x 174 mm.) Inscribed, lower right: *Eug. Delacroix, 1826.*

LYMAN ALLYN MUSEUM, New London, Conn.

The story of the Doge who conspired against the Republic of Venice and was executed by the patricians was the subject of Byron's tragedy, *Marino Faliero*, written in 1820 and performed the following year. On this theme Delacroix executed in 1826 the canvas that he exhibited in the Salon the following year and that now belongs to the Wallace Collection. This study, showing the figure at the bottom of the Grand Staircase, may be one of the sketches referred to in the *Delacroix Sale Catalogue* of 1864 (no. 315).

Pl. 76

FERDINAND VICTOR EUGÈNE DELACROIX

1798-1863

The Lovers

Wash; 8¹¹⁄₁₆ x 7¼ in. (220 x 183 mm.) *Date: c.1830.*

DETROIT INSTITUTE OF ARTS, Detroit, Mich.

The *Hamlet* and *Faust* illustrations that Delacroix did were bitterly reviled in his day, but have been much appreciated in our own. Less familiar are his drawings for some of the novels of Sir Walter Scott, whose historical romances enjoyed great popularity in France.

The Lovers illustrates an episode from Scott's *Bride of Lammermoor* (Chapter XXIX). A lithograph of the drawing (Robaut, A., *L'Œuvre . . .*, no. 305) dated 1830, is inscribed with the legend: *Et l'oiseau tomba aux pieds de Lucie dont la robe fut tachée de quelques gouttes de sang.*

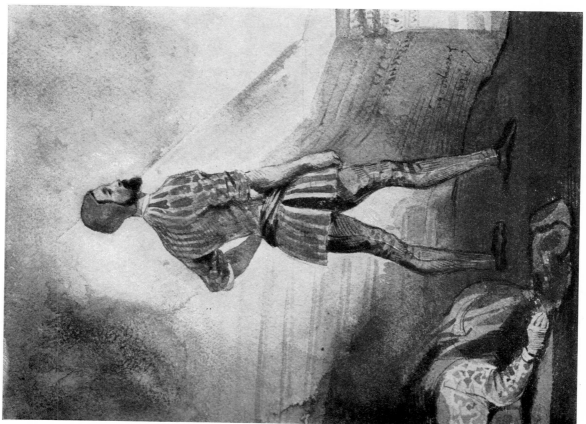

Pl. 77

FERDINAND VICTOR EUGÈNE DELACROIX

1798-1863

Women of Algiers

Pencil; 8⁹⁄₁₆ x 13¼ in. (207 x 334 mm.) *Date:* 1832.

(Rosenwald Collection), NATIONAL GALLERY OF ART, Washington, D. C.

Collections: Kerrigan.

Bibliography: Robaut, A., *L'oeuvre complet d'Eugène Delacroix*, Paris, 1885, pp. 53-4, no. 1629. *Esther Slater Kerrigan Collection Sale Catalogue*, Parke Bernet, New York, 1942, no. 254.

Exhibited: San Francisco, California Palace of Legion of Honor, 'Nineteenth-Century French Drawings,' 1947, no. 31.

The exoticism that is at the core of the Romantic movement has often been labeled a synthetic element in the work of Delacroix—a criticism not altogether justified and based, perhaps, on misleading evidence. He has been criticized, for example, because in his reconstruction of the Orient he relied not merely on his memory or imagination, but upon carefully arranged stage property. Thus Trenchard Cox (*Wallace Collection Catalogue*, 1933, p. 46) objects that 'by dressing up women from the Paris boulevards in Oriental costumes and calling them *Femmes d'Alger* (Louvre), Delacroix prostituted the spirit of the East and replaced a fine, imaginative effect by meretricious exoticism.' However, a study of the evolution of the painting in the Louvre, for which this drawing is a preliminary sketch, reveals in a most interesting way the manner in which this painting was conceived and executed.

During his Moroccan journey in 1832, Delacroix was given the opportunity, rarely offered to a European of his day, of visiting an Algerian home and seeing Moroccan women in their own domiciles. He recorded his impressions in a series of vivid sketches done in pencil and watercolor (Louvre, *Dessins*, 4185), noting essential details and even jotting down names. On his return from Morocco he made some studio drawings (now also in the Louvre) of what were to be the central figures in his canvass. This time he used his own models, following his original sketches for posture, but omitting details of costume, interior, et cetera. (Cf. Lambert, E., *Delacroix et les Femmes*, Paris, 1937, p. 30 and nos. 8 and 15). One of the figures in the Louvre drawing, done on squared paper, is the same as the right figure in this drawing. The latter, however, is more finished, intended no doubt to serve as the final study before the picture was painted. The final composition shows the figures, transposed, with two other companions, richly dressed in native costumes and jewels, seated in a lavish interior. Such careful preparation would hardly seem to warrant the charge of meretriciousness any more than does Poussin's painstaking arrangement of wax figures in a shadow box. If his temperament was volatile and erratic, Delacroix's sincerity is indisputable.

Pl. 78

JEAN-BAPTISTE-CAMILLE COROT
1796-1875

View of Mount Soracte from Cività Castellana

Pen and ink over pencil; 11 x 16⅜ in. (279 x 415 mm.) Inscribed, lower right: *Cività Castellana 7bre 1827.*

(Paul J. Sachs Collection), FOGG MUSEUM OF ART, Cambridge, Mass.

Collections: Giraud; Duc de Trévise; Gobin; Paul J. Sachs.

Bibliography: Catalogue of the Collection of the Duc de Trévise, Galerie Jean Charpentier, 1938, no. 1. Mongan and Sachs, vol. I, pp. 348-9, no. 650; vol. III, fig. 328.

Exhibited: San Francisco, California Palace of the Legion of Honor, 'Nineteenth-Century French Drawings,' 1947, p. 31, no. 38.

'M. Corot n'a jamais pu dessiner . . .' wrote the popular draftsman Lepinois in 1859, an opinion so prevalent for a time that it was not until 1931 that a full-dress survey of his drawings was held at the Louvre. The critic Laran makes the point that incessantly, for twenty years, Corot devoted himself like a botanist to analyzing the smallest tendrils and vines in nature, all so closely observed that he willingly sacrificed the elements of breadth and style, which his critics valued first. The artist worked painstakingly with pen or hardened lead pencil sharpened like a scalpel, with which he dug almost through his paper. For Corot, opposed as he was to the hasty product of verve and temperament, a drawing was a careful documentation: 'One must not,' he declared, 'have indecision in anything.' 'Le dessin est la première chose à chercher, ensuite les valeurs . . . après, la couleur, enfin l'exécution.'

Robaut lists some ten drawings (*L'oeuvre de Corot,* vol. IV, p. 32, nos. 2621-9) done at Cività Castellana on the artist's first trip to Italy in 1825. Mongan and Sachs quote Byron's vivid description (*Childe Harolde,* canto IV, 74) of Mt. Soracte, the craggy ridge that rises out of the Campagna north of Rome: 'and from out the plain, heaves like a long-swept wave about to break, and on the curl hangs pausing'; it is here sketched with the sharp brilliance so characteristic of Corot's incisive pencil and appropriate to the present subject.

Pl. 79

JEAN-BAPTISTE-CAMILLE COROT
1796-1875

Landscape

Crayon; 9⅞ x 15 in. (250 x 381 mm.)
*Date: c.*1860-68.

BROOKLYN MUSEUM, Brooklyn, N. Y.

Collections: Quincy Adams Shaw; Jacques Seligman.

After 1850 Corot's style develops in sweep and generalization, with precision of line and form giving way to summary impression, subtle gradations of tone, and shimmery atmospheric effects. It is landscape no longer 'rendered' but interpreted in a way that was to have marked effect on the early work of Pissarro and Monet, and later Segonzac, as well as on Hunt and Inness in America.

The *Landscape* is a clear example of that liberation from the literal record that marks the development of landscape painting in the nineteenth century. A more profound and affecting statement of nature is here expressed through a lyric impression that is faithful to the original without being a catalogue of mirrored detail.

civita Castellana 9bre 1826

COROT

Pl. 80

JEAN-BAPTISTE-CAMILLE COROT

1796-1875

A Woman Knitting

Pencil; 11⅛ x 8¼ in. (282 x 210 mm.)

(Paul J. Sachs Collection), FOGG MUSEUM OF ART, Cambridge, Mass.

Collections: Paul Rosenberg; Paul J. Sachs.

Bibliography: Mongan and Sachs, vol. I, pp. 349-50, no. 651; vol. III, fig. 329.

Exhibited: New York, Museum of Modern Art, 'Corot-Daumier,' 1930, no. 40. Northampton, Mass., Smith College Museum of Art, 'J. B. C. Corot,' 1934, no. 22. Brooklyn, N.Y., Brooklyn Museum, 1939.

This is an early drawing (dated about 1830 by Mongan and Sachs) that illustrates Corot's careful use of sharp line to define his form. The numbers are part of Corot's scheme of indicating degrees of value, from strongest to lightest, before undertaking the study in color. The woman is presented as an isolated, self-sufficient figure, set within an enclosed space, preoccupied with a domestic chore, like those charming ladies of Vermeer, Le Nain, and Chardin. The artist dispenses with atmospheric highlights and shadows in favor of a straightforward statement. The unfailing French instinct for the graces of millinery is here revealed, and equally sure is Corot's disposition of the voluminous skirt to build a monumental design. Beauty, as Millet insisted, lies not in the face of the model but in the form with which the artist invests her.

VENTE
COROT

Pl. 82

CONSTANTIN GUYS

1805-1892

Vanity Fair

Pen and wash; 12½ x 16 in. (316 x 406 mm.)

Phillips Memorial Gallery, Washington, D.C.

Collections: Kelekian.

Exhibited: Brooklyn, N.Y., Brooklyn Museum, 1934. Washington, D.C., Phillips Memorial Gallery, 'Guys Exhibition,' January 1938.

This Parisian Hokusai, this 'old man mad about drawing,' Guys was almost pathologically shy, infuriated with Thackeray for printing his name, and later enjoining Baudelaire not to reveal his identity when the latter proposed to write his extensive essays in appreciation. 'The carriage, in an avenue striped with shadows and lights, carries off in a swift trot the beauties who, indolently reclining as in a skiff, listen dreamily to the compliments that reach their ears, and abandon themselves largely to the caress of the winds . . . M. G. [Baudelaire's only designation for Monsieur Guys] draws and paints a carriage and every kind of carriage, with the same care and ease with which a consummate marine painter treats every kind of craft.'

Guys's particular flair for recording the sense of the actual moment, the passing scene, was to mean much to Degas and Toulouse-Lautrec. If his memory is well-nigh faultless, it is his eye, sensitive to every tell-tale nuance of costume, gesture, and carriage, which feeds that rich storehouse.

Pl. 83

HONORÉ DAUMIER

1808-1879

A Clown

Charcoal and watercolor; 14⅜ x 10 in. (364 x 253 mm.) Inscribed: *h.D.*

METROPOLITAN MUSEUM OF ART, New York, N.Y.

Collections: Paul Bureau.

Bibliography: Alexandre, A., *Honoré Daumier*, Paris, 1888, p. 376. Klossowski, E., *Honoré Daumier*, Munich, 1923, p. 105, no. 208. *Bulletin of the Metropolitan Museum of Art*, vol. XXII, 1927, pp. 291-2, reproduced. *Beaux-Arts*, 1 June, 1927, p. 176, reproduced. *L'Amour de l'Art*, vol. 8, 1927, p. 150, reproduced. *Sale Catalogue of the Bureau Collection*, Paris, 20 May, 1927, p. 62, pl. 79. *International Studio*, vol. 90, July 1928, p. 56, no. 374, reproduced. Fuchs, E., *Der Maler Daumier*, Munich, 1930, no. 258a, reproduced. Fosca, F., *Daumier*, Paris, 1933, reproduced opposite p. 62. *European Drawings from the Collections of the Metropolitan Museum of Art*, New York, 1943, II, pl. 42.

Exhibited: Paris, Durand-Ruel, 'Exposition Daumier,' 1878, no. 21. Paris, Ecole des Beaux-Arts, 'Exposition Daumier,' 1901, no. 138. New York, Museum of Modern Art, 'Corot-Daumier,' 1930, no. 115. Paris, Musée de l'Orangerie, 'Exposition Daumier,' 1934, no. 106. Philadelphia, Pennsylvania Museum of Art, 'Damier,' 1937, no. 32.

Daumier devoted the greater part of his life to a daily stint that added up to some four thousand lithographs, cartoons reproduced in the daily press where the grocer boy, the *concièrge*, and the *avocat* chuckled over the comic retort without, as Beaudelaire said, ever bothering to look for the name of the artist. Whether he is lampooning the stuffed shirts, satirizing bourgeois platitudes, exposing political chicanery and the tragic cruelties of the courts of justice, or poking gentler fun at inoffensive human frailties or the foibles and inanities of urban civilization, Daumier's lithographs and drawings are in the great tradition. The domestic dramas, the street scenes, the plodders in a workaday world, the pompous professions, the topers and gamblers, all are there as large as life, the types reflected in the individual.

The Clown is shown caught in the mad urgency of his appeal to the spectators to observe the trick he is about to perform with a twirling bit of cloth. He swings his left hand back, fingers outstretched, to beckon the reluctant world to admire his talents. This is a critical moment, since the spectators' attention must be won before he can beguile them into yielding him his livelihood. Behind him is the drummer and cymbalist, supplying the music of heightened climax to an already climactic appeal. The magic of the sprawling, convulsive, fragmented lines and swipes of wash lies in the febrile movement and the note of forlorn gaiety somehow produced by their total sum, arrived at by no precise calculation but by the cunning intuition of a master draftsman—what M. Claude Roger-Marx has called 'an inexplicable logic.'

Pl. 84

HONORÉ DAUMIER

1808-1879

Corot Sketching at Ville d'Avray

Wash; 12½ x 9½ in. (316 x 241 mm.) Inscribed: *h. Daumier.*

(H. O. Havemeyer Collection), Metropolitan Museum of Art, New York, N.Y.

Collections: Durand-Ruel, Paris; H. O. Havemeyer.

Bibliography: Frantz, H., and Uzanne, O., *Daumier and Gavarni* (The Studio), London, 1904, reproduced opposite p. Dviii. Rosenthal, L., *Daumier,* Paris, n.d., pp. 111-12, pl. xlviii. Escholier, R., *Daumier,* Paris, 1923, reproduced opposite p. 175. Klossowski, A., *Honoré Daumier,* Munich, 1923, no. 397, pl. 148. Rey, R., *Daumier,* Paris, 1923, reproduced. Sadleir, M., *Daumier,* London, 1924, pl. 62. Alexandre, A., *Daumier,* Paris, 1928, pl. 37. Bertram, A., *Honoré Daumier,* London, 1929, pl. ii. Fuchs, E., *Der Maler Daumier,* Munich, 1930, pl. 175. *Catalogue of H. O. Havemeyer Collection,* New York, 1931, p. 185, reproduced. Fry, R., *Characteristics of French Art,* 1933, p. 116, pl. xxixa. *European Drawings from the Collections of the Metropolitan Museum of Art,* New York, 1943, ii, pl. 44.

Exhibited: New York, Metropolitan Museum of Art, 'Havemeyer Collection Exhibition,' 1930, no. 142. New York, Museum of Modern Art, 'Corot-Daumier,' 1930, no. 120. Paris, Musée de l'Orangerie, 'Exposition Daumier,' 1934, no. 146. Philadelphia, Pennsylvania Museum of Art, 'Daumier,' 1937, no. 21. San Francisco, California Palace of the Legion of Honor, 'Nineteenth-Century French Drawings,' 1947, no. 53.

Corot was at the height of his career when Daumier, with eyesight failing from his grinding work as lithographer, retreated from the oppressive city to a modest cottage at Valmondois. Eager for a chance at last to devote himself to painting, he took some instruction from Corot in the use of paints. What pleasure Corot must have felt when he discreetly purchased the cottage whose rent Daumier had found increasingly difficult to pay and sent him the title deed. 'My old friend,' he wrote jestingly, 'I had a little house at Valmondois near Isle Adam for which I had no use. The idea came into my head to offer it to you, and since I think it a good idea, I have had it listed in your name at the notary's. It is not for you that I do this; it is merely to annoy your landlord.'

The sketch is a graceful tribute to Corot, here shown absorbed in his work at Ville d'Avray, which was for many years his summer home. The flat patchwork of light and dark masses, within which the opposing ovals of the figure and the bench strike a note of compact harmony, is prescient of the approaching concern of the Impressionists with Eastern decorative methods.

Pl. 85

HONORÉ DAUMIER

1808-1879

Third-Class Railway Carriage

Composite wash; 8 x 11⅝ in. (202 x 294 mm.)

Walters Art Gallery, Baltimore, Md.

Bibliography: Mongan, A., 'Six Rediscovered Satires by Daumier,' *Art News*, vol. 35, 14 August, 1937, pp. 11-12, reproduced. Marceau, H., and Rosen, D., 'Daumier: Draughtsman-Painter,' *Journal of the Walter Art Gallery*, vol. III, 1940, p. 9ff.

Exhibited: Baltimore, Md., Walters Art Gallery, 1937. Philadelphia, Pennsylvania. Museum of Art, 'Daumier,' 1937, no. 25.

This is apparently the first sketch for the larger unfinished painting in the Metropolitan Museum; a subsequent study is owned by Gordon C. Edwards, Ottawa, Canada. By the use of x-ray and other photographs, Marceau and Rosen demonstrate on the evidence of this drawing and the later oils the means by which Daumier attempted the transition to painting. Struggling with what was for him a new and rather stubborn medium, Daumier sought to arrive at his painted version by modifying and filling in his lines rather than manipulation of his paints. Just below the surface lies the linear framework, the method of approach to composition that was for him as instinctive as breathing.

Pl. 86

HONORÉ DAUMIER
1808-1879

Don Quixote and Sancho Panza

Charcoal washed with India ink; 6¾ x 8⅝ in. (171 x 218 mm.) Inscribed: *h.D.*

METROPOLITAN MUSEUM OF ART, New York, N.Y.

Collections: Paul Bureau.

Bibliography: Fleischmann, B., *Daumier*, Vienna, n.d., p. 53, reproduced. Alexandre, A., *Honoré Daumier*, Paris, 1888, p. 376. Klossowski, E., *Honoré Daumier*, Munich, 1923, no. 61. Burroughs, B., 'Two Drawings by Daumier,' *Metropolitan Museum of Art Bulletin*, vol. XXII, December 1927, pp. 291-2, reproduced. Fuchs, E., *Der Maler Daumier*, Munich, 1927, vol. 1, p. 59, pl. 269b. *European Drawings from the Collections of the Metropolitan Museum of Art*, New York, 1943, II, pl. 41.

Exhibited: Paris, Durand-Ruel, 'Exposition Daumier,' 1878, no. 140. Paris, Ecole des Beaux-Arts, 'Exposition Daumier,' May 1901, no. 142. New York, Museum of Modern Art, 'Corot-Daumier,' 1930, no. 116. Philadelphia, Pennsylvania Museum of Art, 'Daumier,' 1937, no. 30. San Francisco, California Palace of the Legion of Honor, 'Nineteenth-Century French Drawings,' 1947, no. 55.

Daumier did more than two score paintings and drawings of this subject, doubtless persuaded that Cervantes' blast at Romanticism needed reviving in an age of smug gentility. Bryson Burroughs' description follows: 'The Sorrowful Knight is in advance, stiff as a ramrod in his saddle on Rosinante—and Rosinante, for all his decrepitudes, walks proudly as though aware of the lofty thoughts and purposes of his rider, albeit with rather shaky legs. Sancho, on the ass, jogs along a little behind. His sack-like body sags about his hips, his chin rests on his chest, and the ass takes things as comfortably as he . . . There is no landscape, although bright sunlight is suggested by the sharp shadows.'

Pl. 87

HONORÉ DAUMIER
1808-1879

For the Defense

Black crayon and sepia wash; 9 x 13¾ in. (228 x 349 mm.) Inscribed: *h.D.*

PHILLIPS MEMORIAL GALLERY, Washington, D.C.

Collections: Alexis Rouart; Henri Rouart.

Bibliography: Escholier, R., *Daumier*, Paris, 1923, reproduced opposite p. 108. Fleischmann, B., *Daumier*, Vienna, n.d., p. 26, reproduced. Marotte, L., and Martine C., 'Honoré Daumier,' *Dessins de maîtres français*, IV, Paris, 1924, no. 24. Baudelaire, C., *Les Dessins de Daumier*, Paris, 1924, pl. 25. Fuchs, E., *Der Maler Daumier*, Munich, 1927, p. 54, pl. 196c.

Exhibited: Paris, Ecole des Beaux-Arts, 1901, no. 267. Paris, Musée Victor Hugo, 'Daumier and Gavarni,' 1923, no. 63. Paris, Musée Victor Hugo, 'Exposition d'aquarelles et dessins de Daumier,' 1927, no. 27. Paris, Musée de l'Orangerie, 'Exposition Daumier,' 1934, no. 132. San Francisco, California Palace of the Legion of Honor, 'Nineteenth-Century French Drawings,' 1947, no. 57.

The lawyer here plays for once the role of hero, pleading the case for a brutalized figure in the box of the accused. The eloquence of the defense counsel, as he flings his arm back in a gesture that must draw with it the sympathy of the jury, is clearly inspired. His body takes on the poetic grace of his ardor, the head poised like that of a ballet dancer who hopes to win her audience completely in the final execution of a most difficult *entrechat*. The pose is similar to that of the central figure in *Un Avocat plaidant*, owned by Franz Koenigs, Haarlem.

Pl. 88

HONORÉ DAUMIER

1808-1879

Scene of the Tribunal

Pen; 13¾ x 16½ in. (349 x 419 mm.)

(Rosenwald Collection), NATIONAL GALLERY OF ART, Washington, D. C.

Collections: Arsène Alexandre; Durand-Ruel.

Bibliography: Fuchs, E., *Der Maler Daumier*, Munich, 1930, vol. 1, p. 54, no. 201c, reproduced. Klossowski, E., *Honoré Daumier*, Munich, 1923, p. 98, no. 132, reproduced pl. 80.

'He has a marvelous and almost divine memory,' said Baudelaire of Daumier, 'which serves him instead of a model.' That Daumier had often witnessed such scenes as the one shown, even in his early duties as a bailiff's errand boy around the courthouse, is likely enough. Done out of court, this sketch is a brilliant improvisation, as close to the very pulse and sinew of the artist as it is possible to get. On hearing the verdict at the tribunal, the accused has fainted into the arms of the court gendarme. Already the judge and attendants have turned to leave the courtroom, the facts of the case are settled, the defendant is forgotten. The prosecutor is busily gathering up his briefs and documents. With the vividness of a particular instance in court, the drama speaks also of a thousand similar tragedies in the affairs of the tribunal. The scene is quickly sketched and so pregnant with meaning that the artist, searching for the most expressive composition, repeats it in a lower corner, and then a third time in the upper center, widening the focus of vision and, at the last moment, crowning the sheet with half a dozen short jabs of the pen—a crucifixion.

Pl. 89

JEAN FRANÇOIS MILLET

1814-1875

Weary Wayfarers

Crayon; 14 x 19½ in. (355 x 495 mm.)

(Clark Collection), CORCORAN ART GALLERY, Washington, D. C.

Collections: Georges Petit; Defoer Bay; Alexander Reid; Alexander Young; H. S. Henry; W. A. Clark.

Bibliography: Holme, C., 'Corot and Millet' (The Studio), 1902-3, pl. M8. *International Studio*, January 1907, vol. 30, p. 198. Moreau-Nélaton, E., *Millet raconté par lui-même*, Paris, 1921, vol. II, p. 36, fig. 123.

Essentially a draftsman rather than a colorist, Millet devoted most of his energy and talents to the countless sketches that preceded or alternated with his canvases. The present study was apparently made for his friend Sensier early in the summer of 1857, the year of his *Sheep Shearing*, after a dark winter when he had been 'physically and morally in a state of collapse,' working on *The Gleaners*. In a letter to his devoted Sensier, he wrote, 'You reproach me with insensibility to charm. Why, I open your eyes to that which you do not perceive but which is nonetheless real: the dramatic.' The cloaked figure, with the raised arm jutting over the low horizon indicating the road to the strayed travelers, manages to lift the character of the scene beyond the anecdotal to a heightened mood of Biblical drama. The strangers are clearly out of key, intruders on Millet's bucolic setting, which has been derived in part from his early readings in the original of Virgil, and later of Theocritus.

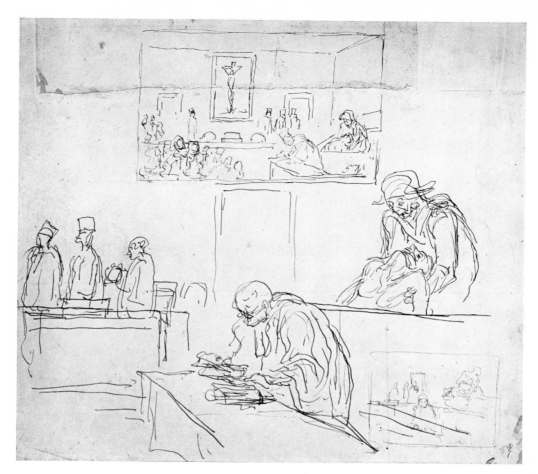

Pl. 90

JEAN FRANÇOIS MILLET

1814-1875

Young Mother Preparing the Meal

Pen and sepia; 8³⁄₁₆ x 6⅝ in. (207 x 166 mm.) Inscribed, lower right: *J. F. Millet.*

NATIONAL GALLERY OF CANADA, Ottawa, Canada.

Collections: Sensier; Moreda; Knowles; Cottier and Co.

Bibliography: Alfred Sensier Collection Sale, Hotel Drouot, Paris, December 1877, p. 60, no. 271. Soullié, L., *J. F. Millet,* Paris, 1900, p. 230. Holme, C., 'Corot and Millet,' *The Studio,* 1902-3, pl. M60.

When Sensier urged Millet to make his peasants more attractive, saying that even village maidens had pretty faces, Millet replied, 'Yes, yes, that is all very fine, but you must remember beauty does not consist merely in the shape and the coloring of a face. It lies in the general effect of the form, in suitable and appropriate action. . . When I paint a mother, I shall try to make her beautiful simply by the look which she bends upon her child. Beauty is expression.' (Cartwright, J., *Millet, Life and Letters,* New York, 1896.) In this rapid sketch of the *Young Mother Preparing the Meal,* Millet has counted on the 'general effect of the form' engaged in appropriate action—the domestic rites of the kitchen —to reveal the beauty inherent in his theme. The drawing is a study for *Porridge* (in the collection of Henry Reinhardt; reproduced in *L. Sarlin Collection Sale,* Galerie Georges Petit, Paris, 2 March 1918, opposite p. 56).

Pl. 91

JEAN FRANÇOIS MILLET

1814-1875

The Spinner (Emélie, sister of the artist)

Crayon; 13¼ x 11¼ in. (336 x 285 mm.) Inscribed, lower right: *J. F. Millet.*

(Gift of W. J. and A. Learmont), ART ASSOCIATION OF MONTREAL, Montreal, Canada.

Collections: Learmont.

Bibliography: Moreau-Nélaton, E., *Millet raconté par lui-même*, Paris, 1921, vol. II, p. 13, fig. 104.

'I am a peasant, a peasant,' insisted Millet, the recorder of bucolic life who repudiated all political inferences in his art. He delights to follow the familiar tasks of the farm and the rural cottage—shepherding, shearing, spinning, sewing, winnowing, harvesting—playing down the sentiment and allowing each subject to speak for itself. Moreau-Nélaton describes the occasion that inspired the drawing: 'Re-entering the house, he surprised the honest girl at her spinning and pencilled a sketch of her at her wheel, called into use later for a little painting of exquisite country quality.' The painting, now in the Museum of Fine Arts, Boston (reproduced, *Catalogue, Museum of Fine Arts*, Boston, 1921, p. 117, no. 318; and Moreau-Nélaton, op. cit. vol. II, fig. 104, p. 123, fig. 175) was engraved by A. Duvivier. Comparison with the actual photograph of his sister Emélie (Moreau-Nélaton, vol. II, fig. 87) suggests the quality and degree of idealization and country grace that Millet infused into his work. 'Submission,' he wrote, 'is the peasant's greatest virtue.' The present theme is saved from sentimentality only by vigorous composition, the sharp silhouette of the figure in studied harmony between the rigid angles of the chair and the implied movement of wheel and distaff.

Pl. 92

JEAN FRANÇOIS MILLET

1814-1875

Sheep Shearing

Charcoal and white wash; 11⅝ x 8⅞ in. (294 x 224 mm.) Inscribed: *J. F. Millet.*

METROPOLITAN MUSEUM OF ART, New York, N. Y.

Collections: Alfred Sensier; G. Louise Robinson; Arnold Tripp.

Bibliography: Moreau-Nélaton, E., *Millet raconté par lui-même*, Paris, 1921, vol. II, p. 36, fig. 133. Allen, J. L., 'A Gift of XIX Century Art,' *Metropolitan Museum of Art Bulletin*, vol. XXXV, March 1940, pp. 57-8. *European Drawings from the Collections of the Metropolitan Museum of Art*, New York, 1943, II, pl. 40.

Exhibited: San Francisco, California Palace of the Legion of Honor, 'Nineteenth-Century French Drawings,' 1947, no. 48.

This is a subject Millet worked on several times in sketches (cf. *The Drawings of Millet*, London, 1906, pl. 35) and paintings (cf. Moreau-Nélaton, op. cit. vol. I, fig. 85, dated 1853, now in the Museum of Fine Arts, Boston; ibid. vol. II, fig. 156, now in the Saltonstall Collection, Boston; also the *Guide*, Art Institute of Chicago, 1932, p. 46, for a third study in that museum). This is a notably successful example of Millet's ability to render the commonplace as a solemn rite, a painted psalm. 'We must be able,' he insisted, 'to make the trivial express the sublime.' The vigor of his contours and the crisp statement of his values here again sustain the weight of his sentiment without trace of mawkish overtones.

J. F. Millet

Pl. 93

JEAN-LOUIS FORAIN

1852-1931

Conversation

Pencil and wash; 11¹⁵⁄₁₆ x 19⅛ in. (302 x 485 mm.)

(Lessing J. Rosenwald Collection), NATIONAL GALLERY OF ART, Washington, D.C.

At the theaters, restaurants, bars, law courts, and drawing rooms, Forain sketched his contemporaries with a kind of humorless amusement. Like Guys and Daumier, Forain worked largely from memory rather than from models. Although in his later years he was strongly attracted to Degas, Forain remains in spirit closer to Daumier, achieving a certain localism of color and setting, but lacking the latter's compositional range or breadth of symbol. Forain's power of characterization is considerable; his line, if not his point of view, is sparing and lacks the flexibility and freedom of Daumier's line. His is a bitter irony without the healing grace of Daumier's explosive humor. One senses his meaning when he said of Daumier, 'Ah! He was different from us—he was generous.'

Pl. 94

GUSTAVE COURBET

1819-1877

The Painter at His Easel

Black chalk and wash on ivory white paper; $21^{11}/_{16}$ x $13^{13}/_{16}$ in. (550 x 351 mm.) *Date: c.*1845.

(Grenville L. Winthrop Collection), Fogg Museum of Art, Cambridge, Mass.

Collections: Gérard; Roger Marx; Winthrop.

Bibliography: Riat, G., *Gustave Courbet* (Les Maîtres de l'art moderne), Paris, 1906, p. 44, reproduced. Fontaines, A., *Courbet*, Paris, 1921, pp. 85, 129.

Exhibited: Paris, 'Exposition et vente de 40 tableaux et 4 dessins de l'œuvre de M. Gustave Courbet,' Exposition privée, 1855, no. 41. Paris, 'Exposition Courbet,' 1867, no. 111. Paris, Ecole des Beaux-Arts, 1882, no. 135.

The exhibition catalogue of 1855 dates *Un Peintre à son chevalet* as 1848. Riat dates it 'about 1845' and calls it *Courbet au bonnet de coton.* It is reproduced opposite a sketch of his sister Zélie playing the guitar and lost in reverie. Courbet is not a draftsman searching for linear essences and tracing resilient contours. His approach is frontal, massive, with few niceties. At the same time he achieves a lyric and romantic note, here fancying himself a kind of necromancer among his magic pots, with something of the attractive diabolism that appears in his portrait of Baudelaire. The crayon sketch of his sister, and the self-portrait in oils, *Guitarrero,* of 1884-5 (in Providence), are similar romantic figures in bare settings, treated with genre realism. Riat quotes Alexandre Schannes' *Souvenirs* to supply a picture of the rowdy gatherings at Courbet's atelier, and that artist's gargantuan preparations for painting a picture.

Pl. 95

PUVIS DE CHAVANNES

1824-1898

La Toilette

Chalk and pencil; 10¼ x 8 in. (259 x 202 mm.) *Date: c.*1883. Collector's mark: 'P.P.C.'

MILLS COLLEGE ART GALLERY, Oakland, Calif.

Collections: Dan Fellows Platt.

Exhibited: Oakland, Calif., Mills College Art Gallery, 'European Master Drawings of the Nineteenth and Twentieth Centuries,' 1939, no. 98. Seattle, Wash., Seattle Art Museum (same), 1939.

This is a study for *Femme à sa toilette*, which is dated 1883 in the Louvre (reproduced, Mauclair, C., *Puvis de Chavannes*, Paris, 1928, pl. 30). This would advance the date, about 1877, suggested in the Mills College *Master Drawings* catalogue. Related to a series of works grouped around the theme of *L'Automne*, the figure in *La Toilette*, done in Puvis's typical classic and elegiac mood, has the massive Greek profile and rounded contours later to reappear in Picasso.

Pl. 96

CAMILLE PISSARRO
1831-1903

Shepherdess

Charcoal on laid cream paper; 15½ x 8¾ in. (393 x 221 mm.)

(The H. B. Hurlbut Collection), CLEVELAND MUSEUM OF ART, Cleveland, Ohio

Collections: Artist's estate.

Bibliography: Rewald, J., *Camille Pissarro's Letters to His Son Lucien*, New York, 1943, no. 36, reproduced. Pissarro, L. R., and Venturi, L., *Camille Pissarro, son art, son oeuvre*, Paris, 1939, no. 1644, reproduced.

Pissarro's drawings, and even more his lithographs, are close to Millet's in their themes of the countryside: fagot gatherers, sowers, gleaners, bathing girls with geese. There is much of the mood and feeling of Millet as well, but Pissarro's statements are more literal and objective than symbolic and dramatic. In 1883 he wrote to his son: 'Rapelle-toi que je suis de tempérament rustique, mélancolique, d'aspect grossier et sauvage, ce n'est qu'à la longue que je puis plaire, s'il y a dans celui qui me regarde un grain d'indulgence.' In contrast to Millet's self-assurance, Pissarro's estimate of his own work, despite his enormous personal influence on contemporary painters, is here reduced to a plaintive note of modesty. The *Shepherdess*, like the rest of his work, must, he confesses, be met halfway to be enjoyed.

Pl. 97

EDOUARD MANET

1832-1883

Woman with Umbrella

Pen and colored wash; 11½ x 7⅞ in. (291 x 199 mm., sight) *Date:* 1881-2.

(Grenville L. Winthrop Collection), FOGG MUSEUM OF ART, Cambridge, Mass.

Collections: Winthrop.

Bibliography: *Gazette des Beaux-Arts,* June 1882, p. 545, reproduced. Blanche, J.-E., *Manet,* New York, 1925, p. 55. Georges, W., *Le Dessin français de David à Cézanne,* Paris, 1929, p. LX, pl. LXIX. Jamot, P., and Wildenstein, G., *Manet,* Paris, 1932, vol. 1, p. 176, no. 470. *Fogg Museum of Art Bulletin,* November 1943, volume 10, p. 26, reproduced.

Sketch made after Manet's *Le Printemps,* dated 1881 (Metropolitan Museum of Art; reproduced in Jamot and Wildenstein, *Manet,* vol. II, p. 101, no. 190). Manet, largely confined to his studios on the rue Amsterdam, had decided upon a series of four canvases in which the seasons were to be symbolized by four women. This one of the famous beauty Jeanne Demarsy, or Spring, and another of Autumn (Musée de Nancy) were the only two completed in his last years. 'I can see him now, bent double, his wrist on the rest, swearing as he worked to reproduce the stuff of a blouse that Mme X left with him after a sitting, a figured silk, shimmering, dainty, beside which it would seem the representation could only be dull. Yet that painting, *Jeanne,* is a charming gem, a bouquet of spring flowers . . . !' (J.-E. Blanche). Manet had undertaken the project with great enthusiasm, himself selecting the costume, elaborate hat, gloves, and parasol; he was to rework the canvas again and again with endless care.

The sketch repeats the spirit of the original, in which the figure merges into a patterned mass of luxuriant foliage. Out of the busy lacework of scrawled curlicues and casual hatchwork, Manet suggests the texture of the costume and the flowery print; while, by manipulating the scrawls in certain areas, he makes the print design itself round out the fullness of the form. For a studio work, the sense of the outdoors is extraordinarily real. Smudges of wash delicately point up the satiny texture of the foliage. The characterization of the head rests on two or three summary notes for effect: the double chin, the dreamy stare, the setting of coiffure under the elaborate lace hat, and the sensual and mobile lips. Jeanne is clearly of that group of piquant demi-mondaines whose bust portraits, both draped and nude, Manet, too ill to paint, delighted to render in brilliant pastels after 1874. (The subject is the last one that Manet etched [Guérin, M., *L'Œuvre gravé de Manet,* Paris, 1944, no. 66]).

Pl. 98

EDOUARD MANET
1832-1883

The Rue Mosnier

Pencil and brush with India ink on wove paper; 10¹⁵⁄₁₆ x 17⅜ in. (277 x 439 mm.) Inscribed, lower right: *E.M.*

ART INSTITUTE OF CHICAGO, Chicago, Ill.

Collections: Jacques Doucet; Mrs. Alice H. Patterson.

Bibliography: Rewald, J., in *Paysages de Paris*, Paris, 1937, p. 19, reproduced. *Bulletin of the Art Institute of Chicago*, April-May 1945, vol. 39, pt. 3, p. 7. Tietze, H., *European Master Drawings* . . . , New York, 1947, no. 141, reproduced.

Exhibited: Chicago, Art Institute of Chicago, 'Drawings Old and New,' 1946, no. 34.

Even as Delacroix and Géricault use line subjectively, as an extension of their individual emotions, so Manet here uses it as a means of conveying his first sharp response to the immediate impression that his eye records, before his mind has stepped in, as it were, to inform and control the senses. Three paintings of this subject, especially *Flag Display* and *Pavers at Work on the Rue Mosnier*, all offer the same casual impressionist view, hastily recorded from a sharp angle (Jamot, P. and Wildenstein, G., *Manet*, Paris, 1932, nos. 289-91). *The Rue Mosnier* exhibits that curious sense of movement transcribed into patterns of line that was to influence Degas. The left half frankly echoes its Japanese antecedents, while the whole provides a clear statement of Impressionist aim and method.

Pl. 99

EDOUARD MANET
1832-1883

Study of Snails

Ink and watercolor; 7⅛ x 4½ in. (181 x 114 mm.) *Date: c.*1880.

(Gift of Robert Allerton), ART INSTITUTE OF CHICAGO, Chicago, Ill.

Some of Manet's sketches retain a childlike quality of incomplete impression: the *suggestion* of a cat crouches under the *idea* of a chair. He hates to mar the whiteness of his paper. A *croquis* of a group of children will run to a bit of hatched pencil work, some flat planes, a glimpse of surface contained within the meagerest of contours, barely enough to secure recognition. A pencil, Chinese brush, or reed pen will call up just enough to convey a woodland scene, a half-seen bird on a twig; or frail lines and a bit of colored wash will bring forth a *Study of Snails*.

If Manet is not a great draftsman, it is because for him form exists as color rather than as line. Yet even his summary notes in graphite or ink are dappled with light and color: the heavy and light darks and the white of the paper are used together to suggest the appearance of half-seen forms in glimmering atmosphere. His pencil sketches are, however, rarely intended as studies for paintings, since the latter as well are created on instantaneous impression. Two pencil versions of *Snails* are in the Rouart Collection (reproduced in Rey, Robert, *Choix de Soixante-Quatre Dessins de Edouard Manet*, Paris, 1932, pl. 28). The watercolor study is similar to those decorations sketched on letters, charming fancies with which Manet relieved the tedium at Bellevue, where his doctor had sent him in the summer of 1880.

Pl. 100

HILAIRE GERMAIN EDGAR DEGAS

1834-1917

Studies of Four Jockeys

Oil with brush, heightened with white; 17¾ x 13³⁄₁₆ in. (450 x 335 mm.)

(Coburn Memorial Collection), ART INSTITUTE OF CHICAGO, Chicago, Ill.

A traditionalist by instinct, Degas was politically an arch conservative and aesthetically a classicist. He was to end, however, quite unwittingly, as a radical and revolutionary in his works. Following his trip to Italy, where he copied the Italian masters and Poussin, Degas fell completely under the spell of Ingres. His first large efforts between 1860 and 1865 were historical-genre compositions like *Young Spartans Wrestling* and *Jephthah's Daughter*. By 1866 Degas had been drawn to the pageantry of the race tracks, there seeking the larger order of moving masses in accidental configurations. The spirited tension of horses and riders at peak of training offered a broad proving ground for rapid hand and eye exercises, for seeking out the stroke and line of motion, or difficult postures in graceful attitudes. What was to prove more attractive to Degas than creating arabesques of movement or masses disposed in dramatic harmonies was this challenge to capture the position of the rider's body, the extreme angle of the thigh and knee, the peculiar sag of the frame at once yielding and in perfect control.

Pl. 101

HILAIRE GERMAIN EDGAR DEGAS
1834-1917

A Young Woman in Street Costume of the Time

Brush drawing in oil heightened with white on brown paper; 12¾ x 9⅞ in. (323 x 250 mm.)
Date: 1867-72.

(Paul J. Sachs Collection), Fogg Museum of Art, Cambridge, Mass.

Collections: Durand-Ruel; Paul J. Sachs.

Bibliography: Boussod, J., *Vingt Dessins de Degas*, 1861-96, Paris, n.d., pl. II.
Mongan and Sachs, vol. I, p. 360, no. 669; vol. III, fig. 345.

Exhibited: Cambridge, Mass., Fogg Museum of Art, 'French Painting of the Nineteenth and Twentieth Centuries,' 1929, no. 33. St. Louis, Mo., City Art Museum, 1932. Northampton, Mass., Smith College Museum of Art, 'Edgar Degas,' 1933, no. 26. Boston, Museum of Fine Arts, 'Independent Painters of Nineteenth-Century Paris,' 1935, no. 122. Philadelphia, Pennsylvania Museum of Art, 'Degas,' 1936, no. 76. Brooklyn, N. Y., Brooklyn Museum, 1939.

'Nothing in art should resemble an accident, not even movement,' wrote Degas. It is a conviction not to be confused with his seizing the casual or accidental in the scene itself. The momentary appearance once chosen, everything else, as in this study in motion, must be achieved with deliberation and finality: the episode and epoch made to yield at once all their possibilities for profound characterization.

Pl. 102

HILAIRE GERMAIN EDGAR DEGAS
1834-1917

Sketch of Edouard Manet

Pencil on buff paper; 12¾ x 9¾ in. (323 x 247 mm.) Inscribed, lower left: *Degas.*

METROPOLITAN MUSEUM OF ART, New York, N. Y.

Bibliography: Catalogue of the Second Degas Sale, Galerie Georges Petit, Paris, December 1918, no. 210.
European Drawings from the Collections of the Metropolitan Museum of Art, New York, 1943, II, pl. 50.

It was owing in part to many arguments with his friend Manet at the Café Guerbois that Degas decided to break away from academic genre and historical painting. The friendship virtually ceased after Manet cut away a portion of the double portrait that Degas had painted of the artist with his wife at the piano in the informal setting of their apartment. This is one of the series of studies (two others are in the Metropolitan Museum of Art, two in the collection of Ernest Rouart, and another in the Fogg Museum of Art) that Degas sketched in preparation for the etching of 1864 (Delteil, *Le Peintre-Graveur Illustré*, vol. IX, Paris, 1919, nos. 14, 15, 16). In one of these the artist is seated, with his top hat on the floor in the foreground (Rivière, *Les Dessins de Degas*, Paris, 1922, pl. 60).

Manet, like Degas, was an exquisite revolutionary, a wit and dandy, close friend of the esthete George Moore, as fastidious in his manners as he was meticulous in the correctness of his clothes, fond of the society that later hooted at his paintings. Fantin-Latour called Manet's a 'true Gallic head.' The face is mobile, revealing a temperament at once exuberant and ready to take deep offense at any slight to his person or his work.

Pl. 103

HILAIRE GERMAIN EDGAR DEGAS

1834-1917

Study for the *Portrait of Madame Hertel* (*La Dame aux chrysanthèmes*)

Pencil; 14 x 9⅛ in. (355 x 231 mm.) *Date:* 1865. Inscribed, lower right: *Degas.*

(Paul J. Sachs Collection), Fogg Museum of Art, Cambridge, Mass.

Collections: Paul Rosenberg; Paul J. Sachs.

Bibliography: Catalogue of the First Degas Sale, Galerie Georges Petit, Paris, May 1918, no. 312. Rivière, H., ed., *Les Dessins de Degas*, Paris, 1922-3, pl. 59. Pope, A., 'The New Fogg Museum—The Collection of Drawings,' *Arts*, vol. XII, July 1927, pp. 25-8, reproduced. *Fogg Museum of Art Handbook*, Cambridge, 1931, p. 112, reproduced. Mongan, A., 'Portrait Studies by Degas in American Collections,' *Bulletin of the Fogg Art Museum*, 1932, vol. 1, no. 4, p. 65, reproduced. Burroughs, L., 'Degas in the Havemeyer Collection,' *Bulletin of the Metropolitan Museum of Art*, 1932, vol. XXVII, no. 5, p. 145. Mongan and Sachs, vol. I, pp. 358-9, no. 667; vol. III, fig. 343. Tietze, H., *European Master Drawings* . . . , New York, 1947, no. 144, reproduced.

Exhibited: Cambridge, Mass., Fogg Museum of Art, 'French Painting of the Nineteenth and Twentieth Centuries,' 1929, no. 34. New York, Jacques Seligman, 'Drawings by Degas,' 1930, no. 19. St. Louis, Mo., City Art Museum, 1932. Pittsburgh, Pa., Junior League, 'Old Master Drawings,' 1933, no. 31. Boston, Museum of Fine Arts, 'Independent Painters of Nineteenth-Century Paris,' 1935, no. 120. Philadelphia, Pennsylvania Museum of Art, 'Degas,' 1936, no. 69. Paris, Musée de l'Orangerie, 'Degas,' 1937, no. 37. Brooklyn, N. Y., Brooklyn Museum, 1939.

Degas, more than anyone else in his period, succeeded in rendering those national qualities and traits of character that are peculiarly France's: her good taste and exquisite tact, her singular charm and sensibility. Invariably, as in *Madame Hertel*, his portraits reflect more than local color and time; they embody those essential gestures and characteristics that are, like family resemblances, immediately recognizable. It is done with a line at once faithful to the original and possessed of an abstract beauty of its own, quite independent of the subject. Thus Degas extends the thread on which hang those pearls of French portraiture by her masters, from Fouquet and the Clouets down through Watteau, La Tour, David, and Ingres.

Pl. 104

HILAIRE GERMAIN EDGAR DEGAS

1834-1917

Duke of Morbilli

Black crayon on white paper; 11¾ x 8⅝ in. (298 x 218 mm.) *Date:* 1867.

THE MUSEUM OF FINE ARTS, Boston, Mass.

Collections: René de Gas.

Bibliography: Catalogue vente René de Gas, Paris, 1927, no. 9. *Bulletin of the Museum of Fine Arts*, Boston, 1932, vol. XXX, p. 44. Mongan, A., *Bulletin of the Fogg Museum*, Cambridge, 1932, vol. I: 4, pp. 63-5, reproduced. *Degas*, Philadelphia Museum of Art, 1936, no. 72, reproduced.

Exhibited: Philadelphia, Philadelphia Museum of Art, 'Degas,' 1936, no. 72.

A study of the duke, for the double portrait of Degas's cousin and brother-in-law, Edmondo, Duke of Morbilli, and the latter's wife, Thérèse de Gas, Duchess of Morbilli, also owned by the Museum of Fine Arts, Boston. (Another oil portrait is in the Chester Dale Collection, National Gallery, Washington, D.C.) The painting is generally dated about 1867. Degas drew away more and more from the society of his friends, and for serious portraiture usually turned to members of his family. In the sketch the head is more gentle than that in the painting, which, in addition to the sinister bent of the aristocratic nose, shows a heavier-lidded, shrewder pair of eyes. The nose he has repeated in the upper left corner, studying the accent of planes on bridge and nostril.

Pl. 105

HILAIRE GERMAIN EDGAR DEGAS
1834-1917

Dancer Adjusting Her Slipper

Pencil and white chalk on pink paper; 12⅞ x 9⅝ in. (327 x 243 mm.) Inscribed: *Degas.*

(H. O. Havemeyer Collection), METROPOLITAN MUSEUM OF ART, New York, N. Y.

Collections: H. O. Havemeyer.

Bibliography: European Drawings from the Collections of the Metropolitan Museum of Art, New York, 1943, II, pl. 55.

Exhibited: New York, Metropolitan Museum of Art, 'Havemeyer Collection Exhibition,' 1930, no. 160. Washington, D.C., Phillips Memorial Gallery, 'Degas Prints and Drawings,' 1947.

This unpublished study for *Les Danseuses au piano* (reproduced, Lafond, P., *Degas*, Paris, 1918, vol. I, p. 63) lends added support for the date (1874) assigned by Mongan and Sachs to the related drawing of the *Dancer Facing Three-Quarters Front* in the Fogg Museum of Art, a study for one of the figures in *La Classe de danse* (Camondo Collection, the Louvre). In the painting *Les Danseuses au piano*, the right hand of the dancer adjusting her slipper rests against the side of a piano, on which is perched another dancer whose contorted arm reaches up her back to scratch between the shoulder blades. The Cambridge and New York drawings are done in the same manner and media, on pink paper of slightly different size. In the latter the artist has jotted down, 'le bras est enfoncé un peu dans la mousseline,' a direction he carried out in the painting that is signed and dated 1874. The figure on the piano occurs also in *La Classe de danse*. Like this one, or the recurring figure of the yawning dancer, the composition of the *Dancer Adjusting Her Slipper* was one that Degas reverted to again in 1878, as the central figure in *Three Dancers* (formerly in the collection of Henri Rouart), and a third time toward 1900 in a pastel *Dancers behind the Scenes* (Meier-Graefe, J., *Degas*, pls. XLIX and XCIX).

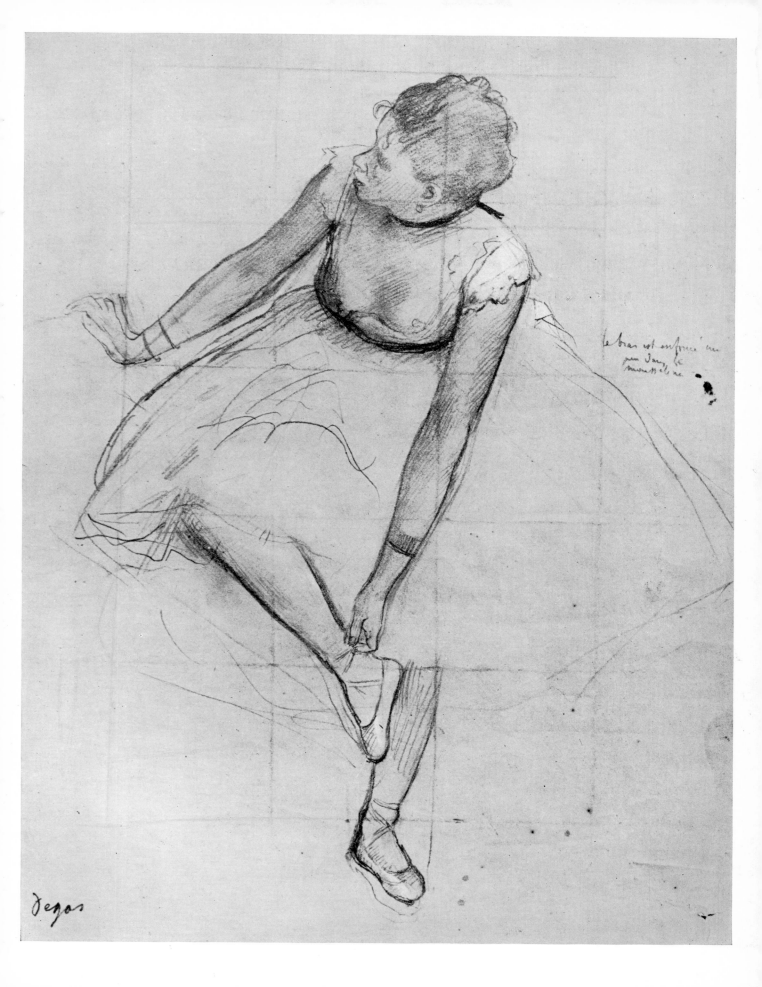

Degas

Pl. 106

HILAIRE GERMAIN EDGAR DEGAS
1834-1917

The Bather

Pastel; 22 x 18¾ in. (558 x 476 mm.) *Date: c.*1890. Inscribed: *Degas.*

(H. O. Havemeyer Collection), Metropolitan Museum of Art, New York, N. Y.

Collections: Tadamasa Hayashi.

Bibliography: Tadamasa Hayashi Collection Sale Catalogue, New York, 1913, no. 85. *Der Cicerone*, Leipzig, 1913, p. 192.

Exhibited: New York, Metropolitan Museum of Art, 'Exhibition of the Havemeyer Collection,' 1929, no. 152.

The queer animal-like movements of models in the unself-conscious privacy of their baths, the simian twist of their limbs in the act of sponging and drying, the interplay of planes on rounded contours, the texture and resilience of flesh, these Degas studied and rendered with what Paul Valéry has called a kind of religious devotion. From New Orleans in 1872 Degas had written: 'I have just failed with a large pastel and feel a certain sense of mortification.' Apparently from the very beginning, as Rouart shows (*Degas à la recherche de sa technique*, Paris, 1945), the artist sought by every means to vary the appearance and often the media of different parts of the same picture. Gouaches and thin dry oils were interpolated in pastels; often he steamed his pastels, working them into a paste with his brush. Always he sought new effects. Vollard (in *Degas*, Paris, 1924, pp. 68-9) quotes him as saying that he bleached the color out of his pastels by soaking them over and over and then putting them in the sun to dry, thus getting a mat finish with luminous undertones. The pose is repeated in another study of a bather, reproduced in *Degas*, Galerie d'Estampes, Paris, n.d., pl. 22.

Pl. 107

PAUL CÉZANNE
1839-1906

Anatomical Figure (Study of Houdon's *Écorché*)

Pencil; 10¾ x 8¼ in. (273 x 210 mm.) *Date: c.*1888-95.

(Lillie P. Bliss Collection), MUSEUM OF MODERN ART, New York, N. Y.

Collections: Georges Bernheim; Bernheim-Jeune; Montross Gallery; Lillie P. Bliss.

Bibliography: Lillie P. Bliss Collection, Museum of Modern Art, New York, 1934, pl. 18b. *Cubism and Abstract Art,* Museum of Modern Art, New York, 1936, no. 39, reproduced. Venturi, L., *Cézanne, son art—son oeuvre,* Paris, 1936, no. 1452, vol. II, pl. 373.

Exhibited: Detroit, Mich., Detroit Institute of Arts, 'Masterpieces of Nineteenth and Twentieth Century French Drawing,' 1941, no. 1. New York, Museum of Modern Art, 'Modern Drawings,' 1944. (Circulating Exhibition: 'Drawings in the Collection of the Museum of Modern Art.')

Intent on making of Impressionism something 'solid and durable, like the art of the museums,' Cézanne turned from considerations of momentary impression to penetrate and record the essence of things, the verities below surface appearance. At the museums the artist made numerous sketches after sculptures, Pigalle's *Mercury*, Puget's *Perseus Freeing Andromeda*, Michelangelo's *Slave*, or, in this instance, a plaster cast of Houdon's *Flayed Figure* at the Ecole des Beaux-Arts, Paris. Another version, having less emphasis on the raw muscular substructure, is in Breslau.

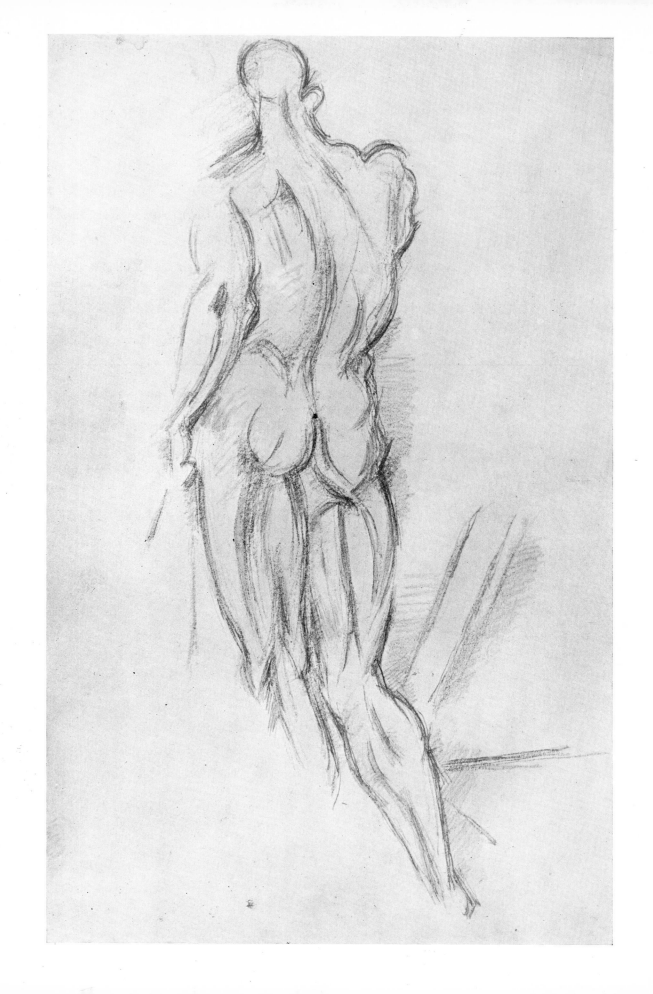

Pl. 108

PAUL CÉZANNE

1839-1906

The Card Player

Pencil and water color; 20⅜ x 14½ in. (517 x 367 mm.) *Date: c.*1892.

Rhode Island School of Design Museum, Providence, R. I.

Collections: Jacques Seligman; Mrs. Murray S. Danforth.

Bibliography: Vollard, A., *Paul Cézanne,* Paris, 1914, p. 47. Bertram, A., *Cézanne,* London, 1929, pl. 6. Venturi, L., *Cézanne,* Paris, 1936, no. 1086.

Exhibited: New York, Jacques Seligman,'Watercolors by Cézanne,' 1933, no. 7. Philadelphia, Philadelphia Museum of Art, 'Cézanne's Works,' 1934, no. 48. Buffalo, N. Y., Albright Art Gallery, 'Master Drawings,' 1935, pl. 124.

A study for the figure on the right in *Card Players,* a pyramidal composition of figures grouped about a card table. The individual player, massive and durable, confirms and reasserts the sense of solidity and permanence achieved by the ensemble. Another study in pencil, almost identical but apparently preliminary to this, is in the Honolulu Academy of Fine Arts (not in Venturi). Both are closer to the Stephen Clark painting than to the version in the Barnes Foundation (Venturi, nos. 559, 560).

Pl. 109

PAUL CÉZANNE

1839-1906

Spring Woods

Watercolor; 15¼ x 11 in. (388 x 279 mm.) *Date*: 1883-7.

ALBRIGHT ART GALLERY, Buffalo, N. Y.

Collections: John Quinn; Cornelius Sullivan.

Bibliography: Quinn, J., *Collection of Paintings, Water Colors, Drawings and Sculpture,* New York, 1926, pp. 7, 38, reproduced. Venturi, L., *Cézanne, son art—son oeuvre,* Paris, 1936, vol. 1, p. 259, no. 959; vol. 2, pl. 292.

This was sketched at that phase of his most mature period when Cézanne was painting scores of meadow or woodland scenes, such as *Normandy Farm* in the Marshall Field collection. Working out the geometry of planes and solids, Cézanne necessarily used his pencil to define the structural lines. It was only after countless trials that he turned from these to build up the same solidity by means of tonal values.

Pl. 110

PAUL CÉZANNE

1839-1906

The Village of L'Estaque

Pencil; 11¹⁵⁄₁₆ x 18³⁄₁₆ in. (303 x 460 mm.)
Date: c.1885-95.

(Gift of Dr. Gustav Radeke), RHODE ISLAND
SCHOOL OF DESIGN MUSEUM, Providence, R. I.

Collections: Radeke.

Bibliography: Venturi, L., *Cézanne, son art—son
oeuvre*, Paris, 1936, vol. 1, no.
1503, p. 328. *Bulletin*, Rhode
Island School of Design, vol. XXI,
no. 4, October 1933, pp. 49-52,
reproduced.

In more than ten studies Cézanne sought from a
variety of vistas to seize hold upon L'Estaque, the
cluster of homes nestled above the gulf of Mar-
seilles. By the use of interlaced, geometric planes
and with almost no use of shading, he strove to
render its plastic essence, its ageless and enduring
solidity. Already in these first tentative notes the
conception of the design is grasped; the play of
light and air, so pervasive in Monet's study, is subordinated to the balance of supporting weights, the
cubicles rising out of the mountain fastness.

It was an attempt, as he explained, to 'realize his
sensations,' probing beyond the surface to the
density and mass below, the organic structure; and
by abstracting its formal patterns, he aimed at
presenting an aspect of the eternal within the particular landscape, the permanent within the momentary impression. It was in response to his own
needs that Cézanne sought to restate the relation-
ship, to discover in appearances 'some underlying
structural unity which answered a profound demand of the spirit . . . without missing the infinity of nature, the complexity and richness of its
vibrations . . . to build that solidly and articulately
co-ordinated unity in which the spirit can rest
satisfied.'

196

Pl. 111

CLAUDE MONET

1840-1926

Boat on a Beach

Pencil; 6⁷⁄₈ x 12¼ in. (174 x 311 mm.)
Date: c.1865.

JOHN REWALD, New York, N. Y.

Collections: Sagot; A. Conger Goodyear.

Bibliography: Rewald, J., *History of Impressionism*, New York, 1946, p. 113,
reproduced.

Exhibited: New York, Wildenstein Galleries,
'Monet,' 1945, no. 83.

Having at first been drawn by the broad statement
of Millet, Claude Monet was later deeply impressed
by the bold ordering of masses and the rough texture of Courbet's method. On a visit to the Normandy coast with Courbet, who was joined by
Whistler, Monet did this careful sketch. Mr. Rewald
reproduces it beside a similar scene done in oil by
Courbet (Smith College Museum); but Monet is
clearly intent on arriving at other effects: the play
of light, the sense of the outdoors in broad sun-
shine, although he has devoted much care to the
structural aspect of the composition. From this
point on, as evidenced in *Harbor at Honfleur* a year
later, his figures became increasingly dissolved in
light. While Impressionism was essentially a landscape art, its sophistication was nevertheless urban
rather than rural. Its city practitioners were concerned with the rapid notation of movement and
momentary patterns of light that could be caught
with pen or pencil, as much as they were with tonal
harmonies and color separations. Impressionist
drawings are therefore more likely to be city rather
than rural scenes. As a landscapist, Monet found
little occasion to draw; his interest in *Boat on a
Beach*, aside from defining the form, lies in flatten-
ing out the solid structure in an airy thinness of
light.

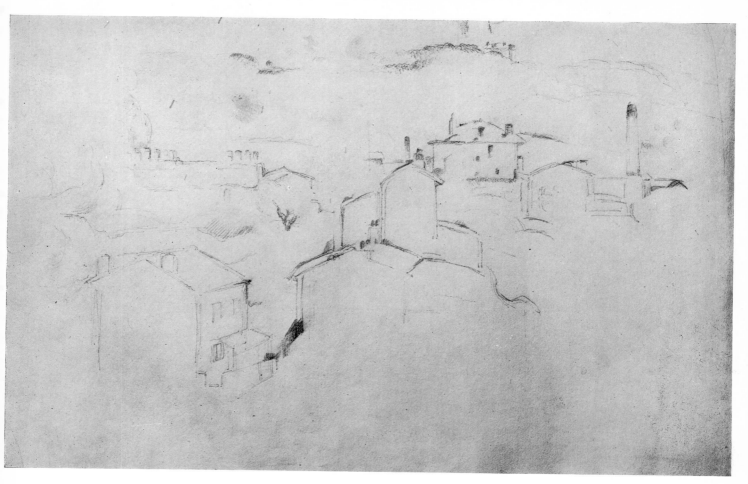

Pl. 112

PIERRE-AUGUSTE RENOIR

1841-1919

Dance in the Country

Pencil; 19¼ x 13¼ in. (487 x 336 mm.) *Date:* 1883. Inscribed, lower-right corner: *R.*

HONOLULU ACADEMY OF ARTS, Honolulu, Hawaii.

Collections: Vollard.

Bibliography: Vollard, A., *Renoir*, Paris, 1919, p. 81. *Bulletin*, Honolulu Academy of Arts, June 1938, vol. VI, no. II, pp. 24-7. Rewald J., *Renoir Drawings*, New York, 1946, no. 16.

This study apparently preceded the drawing in the C. M. de Hauke collection, New York. Both are sketches for the painting *Dance in the Country* (1883), owned by Durand-Ruel, New York. (A similar painting, *Danse à Bougival,* with the figures reversed, is in the Boston Museum.) A third sketch is in the possession of Miss Edith Wetmore, New York. Two etched variants are reproduced in Delteil, vol. XVII, pls. 1 and 2.

Pl. 113

PIERRE-AUGUSTE RENOIR

Nude

Pencil; 18½ x 12⅛ in. (470 x 306 mm.) *Date: c.*1890.

HONOLULU ACADEMY OF ARTS, Honolulu, Hawaii.

Collections: Vollard.

Bibliography: Art News, 26 February 1938, vol. 36, p. 18, reproduced. *Bulletin,* Honolulu Academy of Arts, June 1938, vol. VI, no. II, pp. 24-7.

As an Impressionist Renoir logically began his painting career in emulation of the loose, free brushwork and the melting color resonances of Delacroix. Twenty years later he was to reach a point of satiety, a conviction that he had exhausted the impressionist method, which was proving to be for him a kind of blind-alley exploration. On a trip to Italy in 1881-2, he 'rediscovered' Ingres through Raphael's work, and further sharpened his convictions by a study of the Renaissance frescoes in Florence and Venice. He returned home to abandon the earlier method in the face of considerable opposition from friends. Essentially, the tight, dry manner of his Ingres period was a repudiation of the excesses of Impressionism and an acknowledgment of the primary importance of drawing. His mature work was to begin with a relaxation of the two extremes and a synthesis of warm color harmonies disciplined by firmer line, yet a line that perceptibly wavers and breaks and gives way under the play of glancing light on warm flesh textures.

Thereafter and increasingly, Renoir's figures take on a soft radiance and at the same time a sculpturesque solidity. He is less concerned with the arabesques of line or with the sense of the casual or accidental so necessary to Degas; he makes frequent use of the crouching form and dramatic gesture, although he admires enormously the surcharged immobility of Maillol's rigidly contained figures. But a new ease and economy of line appear in Renoir's drawings, a vigor and breadth of design that dispense with the minor felicities of detail. His enthusiasm for the Italian frescoes is revealed in his later work, and some of the sanguines, touched with smears of velvety black at the edges and drapefolds, appear ready and suitable for mural transfer. Monumental forms take shape as sinuous contours and sweeping masses are sketched in with bold assurance and bathed in brilliant nuances of light and shade. Characteristic Renoir heads—the low brow, the half-smiling mouth, a mixture of sensuous innocence and shy awareness—are set on wise and mature bodies, some of them endowed with a lumbering, almost primitive grace. Such is the bather shown a trifle crouched in the act of drying, set large in the landscape. Renoir frequently made use of the parallel waved line to stress the overflowing vitality of his nudes as they are caught in a shimmer of light.

A similar study on tracing paper was sold at the Jacques Zoubaloff sale (*Catalogue,* Galerie Georges Petit, Paris, 16-17 June 1927, no. 51). A slight variant is reproduced in Delteil, L., *Le Peintre-Graveur Illustré,* Paris, 1923, vol. XVII, pl. 28.

Pl. 114

PIERRE-AUGUSTE RENOIR

1841-1919

Woman in a Rocking Chair

Charcoal and pencil on white wove paper; 14³⁄₁₆ x 11¹⁵⁄₁₆ in. (360 x 303 mm.) *Date: c.*1883.

THE ART INSTITUTE OF CHICAGO, Chicago, Ill.

Collections: The artist's estate.

Bibliography: Rewald, J., *Renoir Drawings*, New York, 1946, no. 26, reproduced. Tietze, H., *European Master Drawings* . . . , New York, 1947, no. 145, reproduced.

Exhibited: Chicago, Art Institute of Chicago, 'Drawings Old and New,' 1944, no. 44.

An impressionist study in curvilinear pattern and doubtless of the period that produced *At the Seashore* in the Metropolitan Museum of Art. Renoir, like Boucher, uses the female form as a decorative motive, in a single elliptic statement fusing balanced repose and rhythmic motion. His charcoal lightly picks up surface textures, and overtones of shimmering light seem to play about the face.

Pl. 115

PIERRE-AUGUSTE RENOIR

1841-1919

Mesdemoiselles Lerolle

Charcoal; 16 x 24½ in. (406 x 622 mm.) *Date: c.* 1890.

JOHN S. NEWBERRY, JR., Grosse Pointe Farms, Mich.

Collections: Lerolle; Durand-Ruel; Jacques Seligman.

Bibliography: Jewell, E. A., *French Impressionists and Their Contemporaries*, New York, 1944, p. 142, reproduced. Rewald, J., *Renoir Drawings*, New York, 1946, no. 65, reproduced.

Exhibited: San Francisco, California Palace of the Legion of Honor, 'Nineteenth-Century French Drawings,' 1947, no. 107. Detroit, Mich., Detroit Institute of Arts, 'Modern Drawings from Detroit Collections,' 1947.

Preparatory study for the painting of *Mesdemoiselles Lerolle au piano* in the Durand-Ruel Collection, Paris (Painted 1886-90, reproduced in Meier-Graefe, J., *Renoir*, Leipzig, 1929, p. 253). How far the Impressionists, following Bracquemond's passionate evangelism for Japanese prints, absorbed the method and the aesthetic of the Eastern artists, is admirably demonstrated in this study with its glossy black masses and refined contours.

Pl. 116

PIERRE-AUGUSTE RENOIR

1841-1919

Judgment of Paris

Red and white chalk; 18½ x 23¾ in. (470 x 603 mm.) *Date*: c.1908. Inscribed, lower right: *Renoir*.

PHILLIPS MEMORIAL GALLERY, Washington, D.C.

Collections: Pierre Renoir.

Bibliography: Meier-Graefe, J., *Auguste Renoir*, Leipzig, 1929, p. 305n. *Modern Drawings*, Museum of Modern Art, New York, 1944, p. 24, reproduced. Rewald, J., *Renoir Drawings*, New York, 1946, no. 71, reproduced. Tietze, H., *European Master Drawings* . . . , New York, 1947, no. 146, reproduced.

Exhibited: New York, Museum of Modern Art, 'Modern Drawings,' 1944. San Francisco, California Palace of the Legion of Honor, 'Nineteenth-Century French Drawings,' 1947, no. 48.

There are two paintings of this subject, one dated 1908 and another done in 1915, and also a bronze relief by Renoir. These might well be three of his bathers again (the lithographic version is so titled in Delteil, vol. XVII, pl. 51) rather than three mythological figures. Where Degas's nudes are patterns of movement, arabesques of action, Renoir's are simply nudes whose movement carries the expectancy of further exposure. The elliptic, cursive lines, the rhythmic melting forms are appropriate enough means for the delineation of goddesses. They are all grace and loveliness; but then Renoir's nudes are generally fit companions to the gods. In the *Judgment of Paris* Renoir has caught the air of dramatic expectancy that is heightened in the painted versions.

Pl. 117

ODILON REDON

1840-1916

Study of a Head

Charcoal; 19⅞ x 14⁵⁄₁₆ in. (504 x 362 mm.) *Date: c.*1880-1895.

METROPOLITAN MUSEUM OF ART, New York, N. Y.

The magic of Redon's world of dream and fantasy lies not in its strangeness, but in the conviction slowly borne in on us that nature might easily at one time have produced just such demon-creatures, and could do so even now. They are not merely believable, but palpably real. One-eyed beings, hybrid animals, quaint Calibans with exaggerated features and limbs, they all possess a physiology authentically derived from nature, so that they claim and win from us acceptance as fellow-passengers on this planet. Redon admits that his method is to copy directly from nature: a leaf, a stone, a hand; then comes the moment of ebullition or intoxication, when nature suddenly becomes invested with another life, transformed into another spirit (Redon, O., *A Soi-même*, Paris, 1922). It is a method that reaches back to Leonardo, the drolleries of Luini and Bosch. Redon put it quite simply: 'My drawings inspire, they do not define. They place us, as does music, in the boundless realm of the undetermined.' Even what might have started out as a commonplace figure, the *Study of a Head*, is subtly transformed, with its hollow eyes, the strange fixity of expression, the nettle-like headdress seen as in a mist, the half-masked visage. She is of that melancholy spirit world so dear to the lachrymose fancies of Poe. It was only slowly that Redon was drawn to this world of half-lights and shadows, when, after a period of romantic Corot influence, he stumbled upon the essential material for his genius, the illustrations that he made for *Dream World* and later for the works of Poe, Flaubert's *The Temptation of St. Anthony, Mephistopheles*, and Baudelaire's *Flowers of Evil*. The pencil had been his natural medium, but the meticulous work, the attention to minutiae which he had lavished on individual drawings, was too readily lost to him with their sale. And so in the end, through the influence of his friend Rudolphe Bresdin, he gratefully turned to etching (1863), and later, under the technical guidance of Fantin-Latour, to lithography (1879). Thus, except for the last decade or two of his life, Redon's work is done almost wholly in black and white. But in whatever medium he worked, as Marsden Hartley put it, 'he has given us a happy suggestion of the reality of spiritual spaces.'

Pl. 118

AUGUSTE RODIN

1840-1917

The Embrace

Pencil, watercolor, and gouache; 12¾ x 9⅞ in. (323 x 250 mm.) Inscribed: *Aug Rodin.*

METROPOLITAN MUSEUM OF ART, New York, N. Y.

Collections: The artist's studio.

Bibliography: Haviland, P. B., 'Principal Accessions: Drawings by Rodin,' *Metropolitan Museum of Art Bulletin*, vol. v, May 1910, p. 127.

The Pygmalion myth readily appealed to Rodin. His friend Gsell quotes him as saying: 'In all that he paints, draws, sculptures, writes, the artist causes his tenderness to overflow. When he draws from the nude he renders her the homage of adoration. By the lines, forms, colors, he expresses his idolatry. He creates a new reality which he caresses and adorns with the most seductive charms, thus becoming her lover as she is his.' (*Twelve Aquarelles*, Paris, 1920, p. 9.) The cool greens and blues as well as the fragmented lines of this tone-poem were in his later work simplified to washes of a single hue as a means of securing volume for smooth-flowing contours.

Maillol preferred Rodin's drawings to his sculpture. 'They are not studies'; he declared, 'they are ideas.' Rodin's particular gift is that of infusing a heightened emotion, often pure lyric or erotic ecstasy, into the nude form. His best means of conveying the mood is by a free, almost abandoned, swirl of contours and calligraphic rhythms that seldom fail to strike a sensual quality. A translucent wash serves to add volume and texture, but only specific enough not to over-emphasize the form. The lyricism is somewhat dated but the method remains wholly fresh and stimulating.

35

Aug Rodin

10.66.6.

Pl. 119

PAUL GAUGUIN

1848-1903

Tahitian Man

Charcoal; 12¾ x 11 in. (323 x 279 mm.)

(Gift of Emily Crane Chadbourne), THE ART INSTITUTE OF CHICAGO, Chicago, Ill.

Bibliography: Rey, R., *Gauguin*, New York, 1924, pl. 19. Rewald, J., *Gauguin*, Paris, 1938, p. 154.

As Van Gogh at last found himself, once he had arrived at Arles, so Gauguin, in revolt against Western convention, discovered a climate and civilization to which his temperament could respond with complete abandon—Tahiti. Here was a primitive people forever poised, graceful, possessed of extraordinary natural dignity; and here in his painting he came to substitute balance for sharp oppositions, to use harmony of line and color rather than tension, subtle modulations instead of violent contrasts. Also here, inevitably, the element of design grew dominant in his work. In *Tahitian Man* he set out to do what he had been exhorting the younger artists to strive for: 'Study the silhouette of every object,' he wrote; 'distinctness of outline is the attribute of the hand that is not enfeebled by any hesitation of the will.'

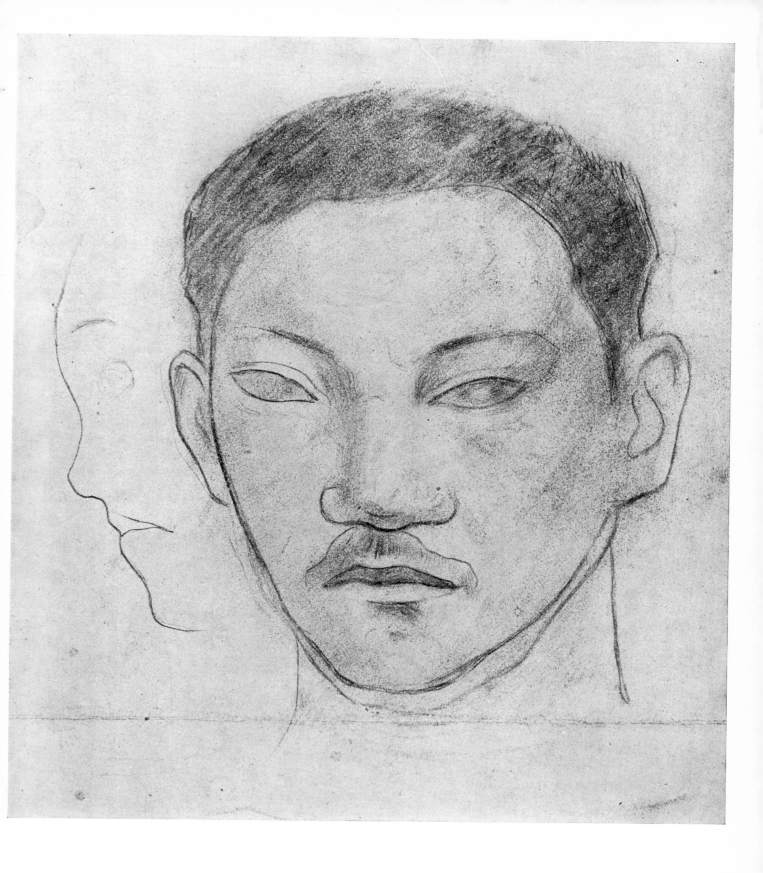

Pl. 120

PAUL GAUGUIN
1848-1903

Tahitian Woman

Pencil, charcoal, and pastel on wove, tan paper; 21¾ x 18⅞ in. (552 x 480 mm.) *Date:* c.1892.

(Gift of Tiffany and Margaret Blake), THE ART INSTITUTE OF CHICAGO, Chicago, Ill.

Collections: Alphonse Kann; Josef Stransky.

Bibliography: Flint, R., 'The Private Collection of Josef Stransky,' *Art News,* 16 May 1931, vol. XXIX, pp. 86, 101, reproduced. Rewald, J., *Gauguin,* New York, 1938, p. 167, reproduced. Tietze, H., *European Master Drawings* . . . , New York, 1947, no. 154, reproduced.

Exhibited: Chicago, Art Institute of Chicago, 'Drawings Old and New,' 1946, no. 20.

Study for the central figure in *Nafea Foa Ipoipo* (When are you to marry?), painted in 1892 during his first Tahitian visit. There is an ease and assurance of line and delicacy of feeling that suggest how readily Gauguin took to his new environment. The area is squared off, the mood evoked in a counterpoint of simplified forms and poised movement. Gauguin's Tahitians seem always lost in thought, meditating in an infinity of leisure. It is that sense of an interior world that we note in Prud'hon and Ingres. As with Boucher, the form is abstracted to serve a decorative end. This figure is used again in another composition in watercolor owned by the Art Institute of Chicago. On the reverse is a charcoal sketch of a Tahitian girl.

214

Pl. 121

VINCENT VAN GOGH

1853-1890

The Bridge of Langlois at Arles

Reed pen and ink; 9½ x 12½ in. (241 x 316 mm.) *Date:* 1888.

LOS ANGELES COUNTY MUSEUM, Los Angeles, Calif.

Collections: Paret; Durieux-Cassirer; George Gard de Sylva.

Bibliography: La Faille, J. de, *L'Œuvre de Vincent Van Gogh,* Paris and Brussels, 1928, vol. III, no. 1471; vol. IV, pl. CLXIII. Scherjon, W., and Gruyter, J. de, *Vincent Van Gogh's Great Period,* Amsterdam, 1937, pp. 16, 61, pl. 31.

Exhibited: San Francisco, California Palace of the Legion of Honor, 'Nineteenth-Century French Drawings,' 1947, no. 134.

In his last years Van Gogh achieved full mastery of the reed pen and used it to catch with extraordinary felicity the quality of a moment that lingered over the countryside on a summer's day. It was a technique won from study of the Chinese quality in Rembrandt's pen sketches, after which the earlier influence of Millet on Van Gogh gave way to that of the Japanese print.

At the time he was sending home drawings like these, for Théo's approval, Vincent was writing (*Letters,* vol. III, p. 53, no. 484, May 1888) : 'This will show you that, if you like, I can make little pictures, like Japanese prints, of all these drawings.' With the drawbridge head like a pagoda, the stately cypresses in an air of idyllic stillness, one might almost expect a rickshaw to come rolling by at any moment. 'I've been worried by the sunset in a study with figures and a bridge that I spoke of to Bernard' (Letter no. 471, March 1888). In the oil painting (Wallraf-Richartz Museum, Cologne) an ineffectual sun appears to the left of the cypresses over the cluster of dwellings.

216

Pl. 122

VINCENT VAN GOGH

1853-1890

View of Arles

Reed pen and wash; 16⅞ x 21½ in. (428 x 546 mm). *Date:* 1888.

RHODE ISLAND SCHOOL OF DESIGN MUSEUM, Providence, R. I.

Collections: Freudenberg; Danforth.

Bibliography: La Faille, J. de, *L'Œuvre de Vincent Van Gogh,* Paris, 1928, vol. III, no. 1416; vol. IV, pl. 148.

All his life Van Gogh had fled the scenes of his failures or pushed on in search of ever-fresh beginnings. It was only when he left Paris and moved on to Arles that he found himself. Here at last in the Crau region of southern France, whose flatness was so much like Holland's, he surrendered himself to its healing warmth, its dazzling brightness, and the peasant simplicity of types such as *Roulin* and *L'Arlesienne.* Shortly he wrote to his brother Théo that his work was completely absorbing him. He was more than absorbed, he became intoxicated by the raw colors whose light broke in on the recesses of his solemn Dutch nature, drawing him on to a frenzied orgy of creative effort.

Van Gogh shared the enthusiasm of the Impressionists for Japanese woodcuts. Writing to Théo, in May 1888, he refers to *View of Arles:* 'I have done two new studies now like this [a shorthand version is here drawn in the letter]: you have a drawing of one of them already, a farm by the high road among corn fields. A meadow very full of yellow buttercups, a ditch with irises, green leaves and purple flowers, the town in the background, some grey willows, and a strip of blue sky. If the meadow is not cut, I should like to do this study again, for the idea was very beautiful, and I had difficulty in getting the composition. A little town in the midst of a countryside all flowered over with yellow and purple: just—can't you see it—a Japanese dream.'

Pl. 123

VINCENT VAN GOGH
1853-1890

The Postman Roulin

Reed pen and ink; 23¼ x 17½ in. (587 x 444 mm.) *Date:* 1888.

Los Angeles County Museum, Los Angeles, Calif.

Collections: Freudenberg; Cassirer; George Gard de Sylva.

Bibliography: Pfister, K., *Vincent Van Gogh*, Potsdam, 1922, p. 37, reproduced. Meier-Graefe, J., *Vincent Van Gogh der Zeichner*, Berlin, 1928, pl. 29. La Faille, J. de, *L'Œuvre de Vincent Van Gogh*, Paris and Brussels, 1928, vol. III, no. 1459; vol. IV, pl. CLIX. *The Art News*, September 1946, p. 32, reproduced.

Exhibited: San Francisco, California Palace of Legion of Honor, 'Nineteenth-Century French Drawings,' 1947, no. 133.

'Last week I did not merely one but two portraits of my postman, a half-length with the hands and the head full size. The good fellow, as he would not accept any money, *cost more* eating and drinking with me. . . My friend the postman for instance lives a great deal in cafés and is certainly more or less of a drinker, and has been all his life. But he is so much the reverse of the sot, he is so natural, so intelligent in excitement, and he argues with such sweep in the style of Garibaldi. . . As for me, I have rarely seen a man of Roulin's temper, there is something in him tremendously like Socrates, ugly as a satyr, as Michelet called him. . . But such a good soul and so wise and full of feeling, and so trustful.' (*Letters*, vol. III, nos. 518, 550, 572, 583.)

The painting for which this is a study is in the collection of Robert Treat Paine, II, in Boston.

Pl. 124

VINCENT VAN GOGH

1853-1890

Grove of Cypresses

Pencil and ink with reed pen on white wove paper; 24^{11}/$_{16}$ x 18^{5}/$_{16}$ in. (628 x 465 mm.) *Date:* 1889.

THE ART INSTITUTE OF CHICAGO, Chicago, Ill.

Collections: Mme. J. Van Gogh-Bonger; K. Fahraeus.

Bibliography: Elzevier's Geillustreerd Maandschrift, Amsterdam, 1905, vol. XXX, p. 230, no. 10, p. 30, reproduced. Meier-Graefe, J., *Vincent Van Gogh der Zeichner,* Berlin, 1928, reproduced, pl. 43. La Faille, J. de, *L'Œuvre de Vincent Van Gogh,* Paris and Brussels, 1928, vol. III, no. 1524, pl. CLXXVI. *Further Letters of Vincent Van Gogh to His Brother,* London, Boston, and New York, 1929, vol. III, pp. 350-51, letter no. 596.

Exhibited: Amsterdam, Municipal Museum, 1905, no. 421. Chicago, The Art Institute of Chicago, 'A Century of Progress,' 1933, no. 880. New York, Museum of Modern Art, 'Van Gogh Exhibition,' 1935, no. 118. Philadelphia, Philadelphia Museum of Art, 'Van Gogh Exhibition, 1936. Boston, Museum of Fine Arts, 'Van Gogh Exhibition,' 1936. Oakland, Calif., Mills College, 'Master Drawings,' 1939. Seattle, Wash., Seattle Art Museum, 1939. Minneapolis, Minn., Walker Art Center, 1940. Pittsburgh, Pa., Carnegie Institute, 1943. New York, Wildenstein Galleries, 'The Art and Life of Vincent Van Gogh,' 1943. New York, Museum of Modern Art, 'Modern Drawings,' 1944.

From St. Rémy on 25 June 1889, Vincent wrote Théo: 'The cypresses are always occupying my thoughts. I should like to make something of them, like the canvases of the sunflowers, because I am astonished that they have not yet been done as I see them. They are as beautiful in line and proportion as an Egyptian obelisk.'

Pl. 125

GEORGES PIERRE SEURAT

1859-1891

The Artist's Mother

Black Conté crayon on Ingres paper; 12⅜ x 9½ in. (314 x 241 mm.) *Date: c.*1883.

(Lillie P. Bliss Collection), Museum of Modern Art, New York, N. Y.

Collections: Félix Fénéon; de Hauke.

Bibliography: Focillon, H., 'Le Salon de 1926, Trente ans d'art indépendent,' *Gazette des Beaux-Arts*, vol. 13, May 1926, p. 259, reproduced. Kahn, G., *Les Dessins de Georges Seurat*, Paris, 1928, vol. II, pl. 63. *La Renaissance de l'Art*, July 1928, vol. II, p. 276. *Art News*, vol. 27, 9 November 1929, p. 17. Rewald, J., *Georges Seurat*, New York, 1943, pl. 36. Seligman, G., *The Drawings of Georges Seurat*, New York, 1947, no. 43, pl. XXXII.

Exhibited: Paris, 'L'Exposition de la Revue Blanche,' 1900, no. 40. Paris, 'Trente ans d'art indépendent, 1926, no. 3221. Chicago, Renaissance Society, University of Chicago, 'Twenty-four Paintings and Drawings by Georges Seurat,' 1935, no. 10.

Searching out elements of like and unlike, contraries and similarities, Seurat sought a subtle reconciliation of light and shade, of complementary colors, tints, and tones. As other artists manipulate their colors, so Seurat labored with his Conté crayon, working up a velvety gloss and infusing a muted vitality by overlaying stroke upon stroke with graduated pressure. In the present study, by juxtaposing subtle variations of light-dark and heavy black, he secures interval values of gray in the hair, and wholly different textures and tones in the collar, the cuff, and the fingers.

Pl. 126

GEORGES PIERRE SEURAT
1859-1891

A Lady Fishing: Study for *La Grande Jatte*

Conté crayon; 12 x 9⅛ in. (304 x 231 mm.) *Date: c.*1885.

MUSEUM OF MODERN ART, New York, N. Y.

Collections: Félix Fénéon; de Hauke; Lillie P. Bliss.

Bibliography: Kahn, G., *Les Dessins de Georges Seurat*, Paris, 1928, vol. II, pl. 91. *The Arts*, vol. 13, March 1928, pp. 188-92, reproduced; vol. 17, June 1931, pp. 601-12, reproduced. *The Lillie P. Bliss Collection*, Museum of Modern Art, New York, 1934, p. 64, reproduced. *Cahiers d'Art*, Paris, vol. 3 (no. 9), 1928, pp. 361-75, reproduced. Rich, D. C., *Seurat and the Evolution of 'La Grande Jatte,'* Chicago, 1935, pl. II. Seligman, G., *The Drawings of Georges Seurat*, New York, 1947, p. 48, no. 6.

Exhibited: Paris, 'Exposition Georges Seurat,' 1905, no. 43; 1926, no. 107. New York, Museum of Modern Art, 'Lillie P. Bliss Memorial Exhibition,' 1931. Indianapolis, Ind., John Herron Art Institute, 1932, no. 109. Buffalo, N. Y., Albright Art Gallery, 'Nineteenth-Century French Art in Retrospect, 1800-1900,' 1932, no. 129. Cambridge, Mass., Fogg Museum of Art, 'French Drawings and Prints of the Nineteenth Century,' 1934, no. 68. Chicago, Renaissance Society, University of Chicago, 'Twenty-four Paintings and Drawings by Georges Pierre Seurat,' 1935, no. 17. Detroit, Mich., Detroit Institute of Arts, "Masterpieces of Nineteenth and Twentieth Century French Drawings,' 1941, no. 58. New York, Museum of Modern Art, 'Modern Drawings,' 1944. (Circulating Exhibition: Museum of Modern Art, 'Modern Drawings.')

For Seurat, who felt that drawing is fundamental to painting, these sketches were the progressive steps by which he arrived at his final composition, *La Grande Jatte* of 1884-6 (Art Institute of Chicago). These structural silhouettes were pigeonholed as essays toward pictorial organization, to be fitted into the final work in the manner of Poussin and of the artist he most revered, Ingres. These smears of black Conté crayon are laid on with the utmost care. Omitting the particular and the trivial, but retaining the individual and the sense of moment, Seurat is intent upon rendering the appearance of volume in space and light. Since there are no lines in nature, Seurat soon dispensed with them altogether, his last contour lines appearing in the *Baignade* studies, as early as 1844. By omitting these lines he does not sacrifice the plastic sense they normally afford, but secures an even richer feeling of rounded surface and depth by allowing the particles of light to play at the edges of the form. For this reason his studies are equally as important as the seven completed canvases that the artist produced in his brief lifetime. The *Lady Fishing* is a calculated study in harmony of contrasts, subtly graded shades of velvety black alternating with masses of filtered light. The figure is stylized and rigid, yet with an extraordinary latent life. And with subtle magic the artist infused the sense of delightful personality and physical charm through mere balance of geometricized elements.

Pl. 127

GEORGES PIERRE SEURAT

1859-1891

At the Concert

Black Conté crayon on Ingres paper; 12¼ x 9⅜ in. (311 x 237 mm.) *Date: c.*1887.

MUSEUM OF MODERN ART, New York, N. Y.

Collections: Theo van Rysselberghe; Charles Vignier; Baron van der Heydt; Alfred Flechtheim; de Hauke; Lillie P. Bliss.

Bibliography: Lhote, A., *Seurat*, Rome, 1922, pl. 20. Pach, W., *Seurat*, New York, 1923, pl. 13. Coquiot, G., *Seurat*, Paris, 1924, p. 105, reproduced. Cousturier, L., *Georges Seurat*, 2nd edition, Paris, 1926, p. 61, reproduced. George, W., *Seurat*, Paris, 1928, no. 3, reproduced. Barr, A. H., Jr., *The Lillie P. Bliss Collection*, Museum of Modern Art, New York, 1934, pl. 63. Rewald, J., *Georges Seurat*, New York, 1943, pl. 87. Laprade, J. de, *Georges Seurat*, Monaco, 1945, p. 92, reproduced. Seligman, G., *Drawings of Georges Seurat*, New York, 1945, no. 56, reproduced.

Exhibited: Paris, 'Société des Artistes Indépendents, IVᵉ Exposition,' 1888, no. 615. Brussels, 'VIᵉ Exposition Annuelle, The Twenty,' 1889, no. 11. Paris, Bernheim-Jeune, 'Exposition Georges Seurat,' December 1908-January 1909, no. 177. New York, Museum of Modern Art, 'Lillie P. Bliss Memorial Exhibition,' 1931, no. 137. Indianapolis, Ind., John Herron Art Institute, 1932, no. 106. Chicago, Renaissance Society, University of Chicago, 'Twenty-four Paintings and Drawings by Georges Pierre Seurat,' 1935, no. 20. San Francisco, Golden Gate International Exposition, 'Old Master Drawings,' 1940, no. 495. New York, Museum of Modern Art, 'Modern Drawings,' 1944. (Circulating Exhibition: Museum of Modern Art, 'Modern Drawings.')

A number of related drawings (Rhode Island School of Design, Fogg Museum of Art) are associated with the concert theme. If they were preparatory studies, the final painting was never executed. In this drawing the angle of the head suggests that the singer is near the wings of the stage and that some more important activity may be in progress to the left of the performer. There is more sense of space, and the alteration of the angle of the male head on the left gives the view a more casual effect than is common with Seurat, while the treatment of the whole is considerably less hieratic.

Pl. 128

HENRI DE TOULOUSE-LAUTREC
1864-1901

Yvette Guilbert Taking a Curtain Call

Crayon and watercolor; 16⅜ x 9 in. (415 x 228 mm.) *Date:* 1894. Inscribed with monogram, lower-left corner.

RHODE ISLAND SCHOOL OF DESIGN MUSEUM, Providence, R. I.

Collections: A. Heymel; M. Guérin; Mrs. Murray Danforth.

Bibliography: Duret, T., *Lautrec*, Paris, 1920, p. xv. Joyant, M., *Toulouse-Lautrec*, Paris, 1927, p. 206. Lapparent, P. de, *Toulouse-Lautrec*, London, 1928, pl. XXXIII. Jedlicka, G., *Toulouse-Lautrec*, Berlin, 1929, p. 333. Mack, G., *Toulouse-Lautrec*, New York, 1938, pl. 27. *Toulouse-Lautrec, Twelve Drawings*, (Pantheon Books), New York, 1945, pl. 12.

Exhibited: Paris, Palais du Louvre, 'Exposition Henri de Toulouse-Lautrec,' 1931, no. 213. Buffalo, N. Y., Albright Art Gallery, 'Master Drawings,' 1935, no. 132. Washington, D. C., 'Great Modern Drawings,' 1940, no. 42. New York, Wildenstein Galleries, 'Toulouse-Lautrec,' 1946, no. 43. San Francisco, California Palace of the Legion of Honor, 'Nineteenth-Century French Drawings,' 1947, no. 127.

'A flat face, a nose that has nothing Greek in it, eyes with a wild light in them, eyelids rather satanical, a heap of reddish hair, flat breasts: that's the woman.' So wrote the Goncourts describing the veteran 'torch-singer' of the Moulin-Rouge, who swayed her devoted audiences with a deprecating gesture or a baleful inflection of the voice that summed up the perversity of a mournful existence.

In his entire work Toulouse-Lautrec comes closer than do any of his contemporaries to the essential character of Hokusai's flat design and simplified pattern. Because the immediate effect of these studies is at once off-hand and anecdotal, there is no suggestion of Toulouse-Lautrec's furious work, the endless hours and countless attempts, night after night at the Moulin-Rouge or elsewhere, to seize the fugitive moment, the fleeting expression and mood, by the barest economy of means.

Pl. 129

HENRI DE TOULOUSE-LAUTREC
1864-1901

Equestrienne

Black and colored crayons and gray wash; 19¼ x 12⅜ in. (487 x 314 mm.) *Date:* 1899. Inscribed with monogram upper and lower right. Collector's mark, lower left: Lugt no. 1338.

RHODE ISLAND SCHOOL OF DESIGN MUSEUM, Providence, R. I.

Collections: Maurice Joyant; Mrs. Murray S. Danforth.

Bibliography: Toulouse-Lautrec au cirque, 17 dessins, Paris, n.d., reproduced. Joyant, M., *Toulouse-Lautrec, Dessins-Estampes-Affiches*, Paris, 1927, p. 236, no. 20. Lassaigne, J., *Toulouse-Lautrec*, London, 1939, pl. 149.

Exhibited: Paris, Musée des Arts Décoratifs, 'Toulouse-Lautrec,' 1931, no. 260. Buffalo, N. Y., Albright Art Gallery, 'Master Drawings,' 1935, no. 131. New London, Conn., Lyman Allyn Museum, 'Drawings,' 1937. New York, Knoedler Galleries, 'Toulouse-Lautrec,' 1937, no. 52. Cambridge, Mass., Fogg Museum of Art, 'The Horse, Its Significance in Art,' 1938, no. 20. New York, Wildenstein Galleries, 'Toulouse-Lautrec,' 1946, no. 48.

Toulouse-Lautrec filled a number of notebooks with sketches of circus performers, popular idols like Blanche Allarti or Anna Bradbury in rehearsals at the Cirque Fernando and Molier. Here rapid movement as an arrested image of decorative pattern suggests at once the particular scene and the poster-symbol. The fragile grace and gay address of the rider are disproportionately incidental to the arabesque of the ring and the contours of the animal. Dwarfed by his puppet-performers, the relentless taskmaster stands with ever-ready whip in hand.

Pl. 130

PIERRE BONNARD

1867-1947

Canaries

Brush; 12 x 7½ in. (305 x 190 mm.) Inscribed, lower right: *Bonnard.*

PHILLIPS MEMORIAL GALLERY, Washington, D.C.

Collections: E. Weyhe.

Bonnard is a highly individual draftsman with a humor and naïveté often very deceptive of the extreme care the artist exercises. At the same time he has gone his own apparently casual and informal way in drawing, using often a grooved line to create a shimmering or mobile effect. But his animals, especially his illustrations for Jules Renard's *Histoires naturelles,* and birds as in *Canaries,* are good-natured creatures, quaint caricatures of their salient bird or beast qualities. Only after a second and third examination do some of these sketches begin to yield their secret charm.

232

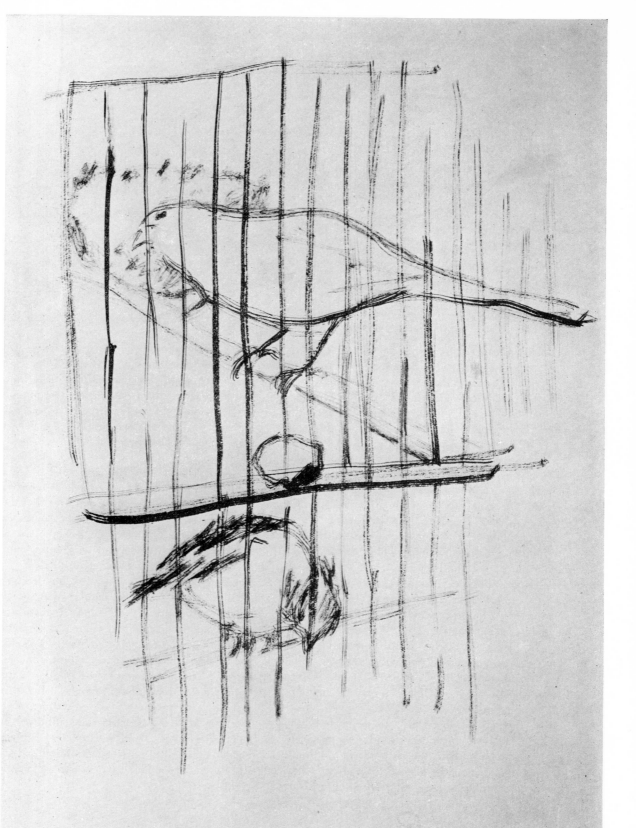

Pl. 131

ARISTIDE MAILLOL

1861-1944

Reclining Nude

Red crayon, traces charcoal on white laid paper; 21¼ x 30¹¹⁄₁₆ in.
(539 x 780 mm.) Inscribed with monogram, lower left.

(Gift of Mr. and Mrs. W. N. Eisendrath, Jr.), ART INSTITUTE OF CHICAGO, Chicago, Ill.

Bibliography: Drawings Old and New, Art Institute of Chicago, Chicago, 1946, no. 33, reproduced.

Exhibited: Chicago, The Arts Club, 'Recent Drawings by Aristide Maillol,' 1932, no. 14. New
York, Museum of Modern Art, 'Modern Drawings,' 1944. Buffalo, N. Y.,
Albright Art Gallery, 'Aristide Maillol,' 1945, no. 56.

In Maillol's fingers the grease crayon molded plastic contours and his studies have the soft rigidity of enclosed volume and modeled substance that come naturally from the hand of the sculptor. Having begun as painter and tapestry designer, under the avowed influence of Gauguin and Renoir, it was a matter of instinct for Maillol to turn to the crayon or chalk to sketch his compositions for sculptures. He rarely sculpted direct from the model, but drew from life and used the drawings to make working sketches for carving. Maillol preferred Rodin's drawings—'ideas' he called them—to those of Ingres —beautiful but 'a trifle cold—office work,' he felt; but in his endless variations on the theme of the female nude figure and his single-minded devotion to its haunting mystery, Maillol is closer to Ingres and the central tradition of Greece. His is a kind of pagan devotion to the nude, so that he comes by his classicism instinctively as well as through training. In his late seventies Maillol remarked that 'Puvis de Chavannes used to say that one who didn't love women couldn't be an artist. . . It isn't women I love, it's young girls. I love the rosy freshness of very young girls who have in their eyes that faith in life, that confidence which no melancholy can mar. . . That love of young girls persists in me. It is even stronger than in the days of my youth. . .' The serenity of mood in his figures, the inner harmony, the amplitude of proportion, the melting

forms, and infinitely subtle transitions of planes, these are expressions of Maillol's love. So sure is he of its purity, that the sculptor finds no need to resort to elongations and distortions to imbue his figures with spirituality; he can rely on the mystery and refinement inherent in superbly natural translations of the nude as they take form under his fingers.

His drawings, like the nearly life-size *Reclining Nude*, have a kind of abstract life of their own; the sense of the model, the pulse and breath of the living original have been interfused and form the link that exists between substance and image. It is a subtle magic that does not depend on gesture or grimace. As a peasant attached to the countryside of his native Banyuls, a fishing village on the Mediterranean, Maillol sensed the quieter pulse of nature herself, the latent powers in her slumbering stillness. So, too, he admired the air of calm and permanence in Egyptian sculptures. 'For my taste,' he said, 'there should be as little movement as possible in sculpture. . . The more motionless Egyptian statues are, the more they seem about to move.' It is this latent activity, this moment of poised stillness, that characterizes Maillol's sketches and sculptures. The sensuous *Reclining Nude*, monumental and durable, exudes the vitality of arrested motion and stirs into life the heavy contour that encases and contains the rigid form.

Pl. 132

HENRI-MATISSE

1869-

Nude in Armchair

India ink with brush on laid white paper; 25⅞ x 18⅜ in. (657 x 467 mm.) *Date: c.*1906. Inscribed, lower right: *Henri-Matisse.*

(Gift of Mrs. Potter Palmer), THE ART INSTITUTE OF CHICAGO, Chicago, Ill.

Collections: Dr. Heinz Braune.

Bibliography: Schacht, R., *Henri-Matisse*, Dresden, 1922, p. 62, reproduced.

Exhibited: Berlin, Thannhauser Galleries, 'Matisse Exhibition,' 1930, no. 107. Chicago, Art Institute of Chicago, 'Drawings Old and New' 1946, no. 36.

Matisse's approach to his subject matter is highly individual, his conception of form thoroughly subjective: his aim is the synthesis between objective truth to the character of the original and the requirements of his own decorative transcriptions. This aim is singularly unchanged in the forty years since he wrote: 'Supposing I want to paint the body of a woman. First of all I endow it with grace and charm but I know that something more than that is necessary. I try to condense the meaning of this body by drawing the essential lines. The charm will then become less apparent at first glance but in the long run it will begin to emanate from the new image. This image at the same time will be enriched by a wider meaning, a more comprehensively human one, while the charm, being less apparent, will not be its only characteristic. It will be merely one element in the general conception of the figure.'

Henri-Matisse

Pl. 133

HENRI-MATISSE

1869-

The Plumed Hat

Pencil; 20½ x 14 in. (520 x 355 mm.) Inscribed, lower left: *Henri-Matisse* 1919.

JOHN S. NEWBERRY, JR., Grosse Pointe Farms, Mich.

Collections: Pierre Matisse.

Bibliography: Cinquante Dessins par Henri-Matisse, Paris, 1920, pl. 14. Salinger, M., 'White Plumes with Variations,' *Parnassus*, December 1932, p. 10, reproduced. *Modern Drawings*, Museum of Modern Art, New York, 1944, p. 50, reproduced. Romm, A., *Henri-Matisse, A Social Critique*, New York, 1947, p. 19, reproduced.

Exhibited: Cambridge, Mass., Fogg Museum of Art, 1934. New York, Museum of Modern Art, 1944. Detroit, Mich., Detroit Institute of Arts, 1947. Bloomfield Hills, Mich., Cranbrook Academy of Art, 1947.

One of a series of drawings related to, and probably studies for, three paintings, namely, *White Plumes*, in the Minneapolis Institute of Arts (reproduced by Miss Salinger); *Mlle X*, in the Chester Dale Collection; and *Woman in a Plumed Hat*, in the Göteborgs Museum, Gothenburg, Sweden. It is a study in elegance and transition—a simple curved line casually suggests the graceful turn of the hat brim, the profiled upper face, the loop of feathers.

Pl. 134

HENRI-MATISSE

1869-

Nude (Nue au Tabouret)

Ink; 24 x 18 in. (610 x 457 mm.) Inscribed, lower left: *Henri-Matisse*, 1936.

FINE ARTS GALLERY OF SAN DIEGO, San Diego, Calif.

Collections: Thannhauser; Rosengart; May.

Exhibited: Paris, Paul Rosenberg Gallery, 'Matisse Exposition,' 1937.

Matisse will alter the proportions of the human form to arrive at a larger harmony of design. Often he restricts himself to the use of a free-flowing sinuous line moving within two dimensions, relying on simple loops and bulges to suggest volume and depth. 'A drawing,' he insists, 'must have a power of expansion which can bring to life the space which surrounds it.' His natural gift is for abstracting the human form in a pattern of continuous flowing line, unrelieved and two-dimensional. There is no weight of thought, no burden of sentiment or symbol; the appeal is to the eye. In thousands of drawings in ink, charcoal, or pencil, he has progressed with equal and perhaps excessive facility from tentative scrawls of landscape to studies alternately *fauve* and naive, playing with dots or loops, tracing contours, juggling graceful designs and rhythmic patterns, sometimes abruptly shattering their too-obvious charm with bravura hatchwork. The distinguishing qualities derived from his kinship with the calligraphers of Persia are revealed in those patterned figures, odalisques, and sprawling nudes that merge and become one with the decorative motives of wallpaper and furnishings.

Pl. 135

HENRI-MATISSE

1869-

Odalisque

Ink; 25¾ x 19⅞ in. (654 x 504 mm.) Inscribed, lower right: 1928 *Henri-Matisse*.

(Lillie P. Bliss Bequest), MUSEUM OF MODERN ART, New York, N. Y.

Collections: Thannhauser; Paul Lamb.

Bibliography: Purrmann, H., *Henri-Matisse*, Berlin, 1930, p. 4, reproduced. Laporte, P. M., 'Humanism and the Contemporary Primitive,' *Gazette des Beaux-Arts*, vol. 29, January 1946, pp. 54, 60, reproduced. Valsecchio, M., *Disegni di Henri-Matisse*, Milan, 1944, pl. 7.

Exhibited: New York, Museum of Modern Art, 'Drawings in the Collection of the Museum of Modern Art,' 1947. (Circulating Exhibition: 'Twentieth-Century Drawings from the Collection of the Museum of Modern Art.')

For Matisse especially, drawing is a way of thinking aloud. His painting generally comes afterwards, but experiments and innovations are done with pen or pencil. So faithful is his eye to the essential form of the original, and so unerring his hand, that he can allow his decorative sense full play without danger of betraying his subject. And always he draws with such tact, and so lyrical and economical are his means, that the spectator's eye is left free to make its own way and participate in the exploration of the design.

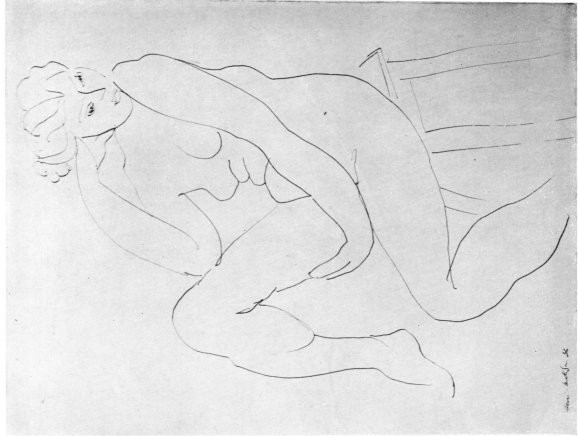

Pl. 136

GEORGES ROUAULT
1871-

Two Judges

Gouache on gray Ingres paper; 25⅛ x 18¾ in. (639 x 476 mm.) *Date:* c.1907

PORTLAND ART MUSEUM, Portland, Ore.

Collections: Pierre Matisse.

Bibliography: Art News, 1 March 1941, p. 34, reproduced. Jewell, E. A., *Rouault*, New York, 1945, reproduced.

Exhibited: New York, Museum of Modern Art, 'Georges Rouault,' 1945.

Except in his early efforts between 1899 and 1903, when he demonstrated in pencil drawings, such as *Portrait of My Mother* (reproduced, Venturi, L., *Rouault*, New York, 1940, pl. 10), an exquisite gift for highly sensitive portraiture of the traditional kind, Rouault has not been concerned with pure linear values or calligraphic effects. But if he has given up much, he has sought more. By 1907, the approximate date of *Two Judges*, he is drawing directly with the brush in heavy outlines, aiming at a monumental and massive definition of his forms, at once crudely durable and subtly variable in textures and tonalities. Deeply moral and religious by nature, as a youth Rouault became a 'social painter,' castigating the prostitution of virtue and justice in a venal social order. With less humor and astringent irony than Daumier, but with concepts already Biblical in character, he shows in *Two Judges* the ugly head of judicial authority, warped, cynical, leering accusingly. Rouault has since matured beyond these jeremiads to a point of view of more detached austerity and a use of simplified forms of sculptural compactness, intense and strangely hieratic.

242

Pl. 137

RAOUL DUFY

1879-

Horses and People

Pen and ink; 14½ x 21 in. (367 x 533 mm.)

J<small>OHN</small> H<small>ERRON</small> A<small>RT</small> G<small>ALLERY</small>, Indianapolis, Ind.

Collections: The artist.

The decorative exploration, the exquisite touch, the assured line moving in the purer realm of creative fancy, these are the marks of Dufy's draftsmanship. There is a lyricism of the eye, a linear wit and gaiety in this rapid sketch, that proceed from no calculated disposition of figures but the lilting mood of the craftsman himself.

Pl. 138

ANDRÉ DUNOYER DE SEGONZAC

1885-

Model in a Chair

Pen and ink on white wove paper; 13 x 20 in. (330 x 501 mm.)

BROOKLYN MUSEUM, Brooklyn, N. Y.

Collections: Crowninshield.

The nude is a study in design with whatever distortions are necessary to achieve a decorative end. Segonzac is a romanticist in his eloquent use of shadowy masses and often not very far removed from the Italian, Guercino, in his use of swirling wet lines and smudges of accent. There is even greater individuality in his drawings than appears in his paintings, and they deserve to be far better known than they are.

The dissolution of subject matter in strong light, by which the Impressionists broke with traditional canons of painting, had been counteracted by an emphasis on structural form in the work of the Neo-Impressionists, Seurat and Cézanne. Cubism followed shortly thereafter, inaugurated by Picasso and Braque in 1907 as the logical extension of this desire to reaffirm the geometric essence of things. Reasoning from this point, artists grew insistent and extreme in their demonstration that the important factor after all was not *what* the artist painted, but *how* he constructed his picture, and that form and color were therefore both means and ends in themselves. Thus it came about that Cubism, which had sought to restore subject matter, inevitably led to a denial of the necessity of representation altogether. The central issue of twentieth-century painting may thus be said to have been implicit in the revolution effected by Impressionism; while the principle underlying non-objective or abstract painting became as radical an innovation as naturalistic painting had been in the fourteenth century. Braque's statement that 'It is not the function of the painter to reconstruct an anecdote but to compose a pictorial fact' (*Braque*, Paris, 1945, p. 57.) echoed and was in turn restated in innumerable manifestoes supporting the broad gamut from Cubism to near and pure abstraction. Within this range Braque functions as a distinguished classicist, whose austerity and reticence have lent the movement its widest authority. In the *Still Life* sketch, the constants are abstracted and set in harmonious relation, with a certain lyricism of form and nicety of expression that are not remote from those of Chardin and Boucher.

Pl. 140

ROBERT DELAUNAY

1885-1941

Eiffel Tower

Ink on wallboard; 21½ x 19⅜ in. (546 x 492 mm.) *Date*: 1910.

Museum of Modern Art, New York, N. Y.

With the advent of Cubism one enters upon another era of painting and it seems fitting in a survey that reaches back to the fifteenth century to take pause with these indications of a new cycle of aesthetic doctrine and taste. A major innovator among the French abstractionists, who are themselves divided into various categories of the left and right, Delaunay may be taken as the measure of the modern movement, for, like it, he rejects all classification as delimiting and false. For himself he declares that he has no liking for schools, theories, or systems: 'Il n'y a que le métier.' He argues, nevertheless, that visual impressions come from 'des contrastes simultanés, forme, métier et tout est couleur en mouvement' (Coquiot, G., *Les Indépendents,* Paris, 1920, p. 182). In these 'simultaneous contrasts' of color, Delaunay turned from the somberer palette of Picasso and Braque to restore the pure colors of the early Impressionists, restricting himself to the music of color harmonies that earned for his style the name of 'Orphism.' The earlier *Eiffel Tower* of 1910, its kaleidoscopic view and simultaneous contrast of semi-abstracted forms and moving lines, carries the germ of Manetti's Futurism in Italy as well as the conglomeration of stylistic experiments that characterize the contributions of twentieth-century painting.

250

Pl. 141

PABLO PICASSO

1881-

Peasants from Andorra

Pen and ink; 24^{15}⁄$_{16}$ x 17^{1}⁄$_{16}$ in. (631 x 431 mm.)

Date: 1906.

(Gift of Robert Allerton), ART INSTITUTE OF CHICAGO, Chicago, Ill.

Exhibited: New York, Museum of Modern Art, 'Picasso, Forty Years of His Art,' November 1939-January 1940, p. 55. Chicago, Art Institute of Chicago, 'Drawings Old and New,' 1940, no. 63.

___

Sketch made during the artist's stay at Gosol in the Andorra Valley of the Spanish Pyrenees, when he suddenly emerged from the mood of introspective melancholy into the luminous serenity of his 'rose period.' This was the year also of the *Self Portrait* and the *Portrait of Gertrude Stein*, in which the mask-like faces are abstracted, lost in thought. The present study is a tentative searching for the note of archaic passiveness that he observed in these secluded peasants.

Pl. 142

PABLO PICASSO

1881-

Standing Nude

Grease crayon pencil; 14½ x 11¼ in. (367 x 285 mm.) *Date:* 1907.

BROOKLYN MUSEUM, Brooklyn, N. Y.

Collections: Paul Rosenberg

Bibliography: Zervos, C., *Pablo Picasso*, Paris and New York, 1932, no, 369, pl. 176.

___

Picasso's development of Cubism stems from his abrupt shift away from classic and traditional influences to a growing concern with abstract aesthetic problems. In 1907 the artist began his studies of Negro art, experimenting with forms which have a non-conventional rightness of proportion that is wholly outside the Greek and Raphaelite traditions. Mr. Barr points to a fusion of Iberian and African influence apparently first indicated in Picasso's masterwork of 1907, the *Demoiselles d'Avignon.* The *Standing Nude* echoes the interest in 'primitive' human forms that Gauguin had stimulated with his Tahitian nudes.

252

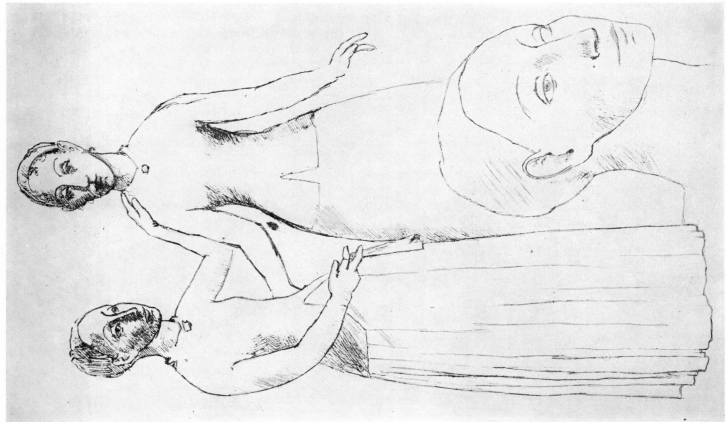

Pl. 143

PABLO PICASSO

1881-

*A Mother Holding a Child, and Four Studies
of Her Right Hand*

Black crayon on cream-colored paper; 13½ x
10½ in. (342 x 266 mm.) *Date:* 1904. Inscribed,
lower-right corner: *Picasso.*

(Paul J. Sachs Collection), FOGG MUSEUM OF ART,
Harvard University, Cambridge, Mass.

Collections: Vignier; Paul J. Sachs.

Bibliography: Picasso, Forty Years of His Art,
Museum of Modern Art, New York,
1939, p. 35, reproduced. Mongan
and Sachs, vol. I, p. 403, no. 741;
vol. III, fig. 399.

Exhibited: St. Louis, Mo., City Art Museum, 1932.
Hartford, Conn., Wadsworth Atheneum,
'Pablo Picasso,' 1934, no. 82. Brooklyn,
N. Y., Brooklyn Museum, 1939. New
York, Museum of Modern Art, 'Picasso,
Forty Years of his Art,' 1939, no. 23.

Study for the painting *Family of Acrobats* in the
Göteborgs Art Museum in Sweden. Of the early
'blue period,' which produced the *Old Guitarist* in
the Art Institute of Chicago, this drawing, with its
unrelieved pathos, is an expression of the *suspire
de profundis* of the artist's sensitive youth. The
gaunt features, sinuous limbs, and angular postures
are expressive of all the sadness inherent in the subjects of this period, conceived at a time when he
quite naturally took to the Mannerist style of the
Spanish artists Morales and El Greco.

Pl. 144

PABLO PICASSO

1881-

Four Ballet Dancers

Ink; 13½ x 10 in. (342 x 253 mm.) *Dated:* 1925.
Inscribed.

(Gift of Mrs. John D. Rockefeller, Jr.), MUSEUM
OF MODERN ART, New York, N. Y.

Collections: Rockefeller.

Bibliography: George, W., *Picasso, Dessins,* Paris,
1926, pl. 46. *Picasso, Forty Years
of His Art,* Museum of Modern Art,
New York, 1939, p. 128, reproduced.

Exhibited: (Circulating Exhibition: 'Drawings in
the Collection of the Museum of
Modern Art.')

One of a series of 'classic' figure drawings in ink
of dancing groups, studied exercises in balanced
linear pattern that express ordered grace and rhythmic movement. Picasso spent the early part of 1925
in Monte Carlo during the ballet season. Although
he had abandoned the 'classic' phase of his career
in earlier months and was devoting his brush to
Cubist still-life compositions, he returned to the
classical style for these dancing figures, executed
with a virtuosity that exceeds in grace and verve anything of the kind previously drawn by him. He has
changed his style so frequently that transitional
drawings are often marked by uncertainty. Mastery
of the form is followed by a departure into other
realms, though he does not hesitate to return to
earlier periods with fresh understanding or a new
synthesis.

Pl. 145

PABLO PICASSO

1881-

Two Figures on the Beach

Ink; 15¾ x 19⅝ in. (400 x 499 mm.) Inscribed, lower right: *Picasso Cannes 28 Juillet* XXXIII.

MUSEUM OF MODERN ART, New York, N. Y.

Collections: Galérie Simon.

Bibliography: Stein, Gertrude, *Picasso*, London, 1939, no. 53. Barr, A. H., Jr., *Picasso, Fifty Years of His Art*, New York, 1946, p. 184, reproduced. *Fantastic Art, Dada, Surrealism*, Museum of Modern Art, New York, 1947, p. 140, reproduced.

Exhibited: New York, Museum of Modern Art, 'Picasso, Forty Years of His Art,' 1939, no. 258. Mexico City, Sociedad de Arte Mexicano, 'Picasso,' 1944. (Circulating Exhibition: '100 Drawings from the Collection of Museum of Modern Art.')

'It was at this time, that is to say in 1933, that once more he ceased to paint but he continued to make drawings and during the summer of 1933 he made his only surrealist drawings. Surrealism could console him a little, but not really. The surrealists still see things as everyone else sees them, they complicate them in a different way but the vision is that of every one else, in short the complication is the complication of the twentieth century but the vision is that of the nineteenth century. Picasso only sees something else, another reality.' (Stein, G., op. cit. p. 43.)

A kind of moral allegory of the vanities and repressions that accompany the public display of nudity on the beach. There is a suggestion of concealing doors and shutters battered away, of old codes and mores crumbling like shattered idols.

256

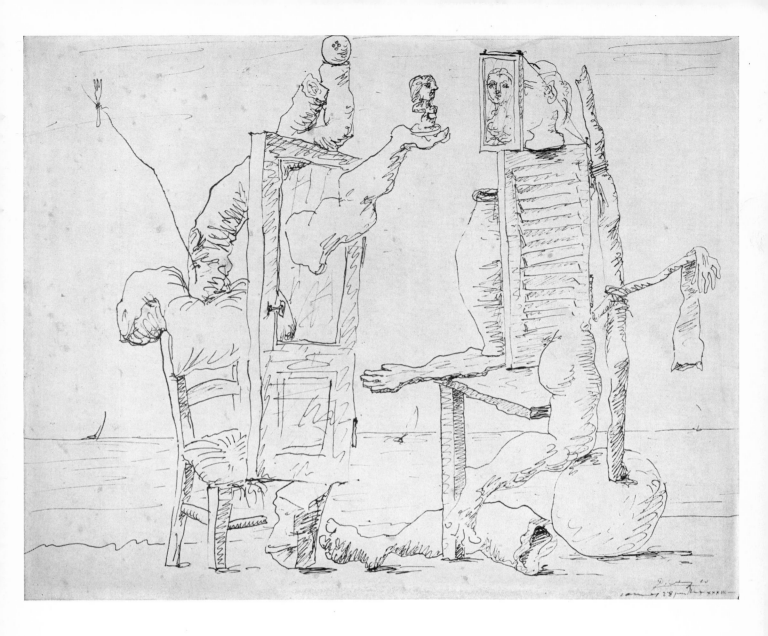